A
SANGUINE
TALE

Unfolding the Life of a Project Engineer

RAJAT

Copyright © Rajat 2022
All Rights Reserved.

ISBN 979-8-88704-866-6

This book has been published with all efforts taken to make the material error-free after the consent of the author. However, the author and the publisher do not assume and hereby disclaim any liability to any party for any loss, damage, or disruption caused by errors or omissions, whether such errors or omissions result from negligence, accident, or any other cause.

While every effort has been made to avoid any mistake or omission, this publication is being sold on the condition and understanding that neither the author nor the publishers or printers would be liable in any manner to any person by reason of any mistake or omission in this publication or for any action taken or omitted to be taken or advice rendered or accepted on the basis of this work. For any defect in printing or binding the publishers will be liable only to replace the defective copy by another copy of this work then available.

CONTENTS

CONTENTS

CONTENTS

PROLOGUE

I heard the whisper, *Yes, he is coming back.* Someone was saying, *move your right hand,* and I obeyed. Then the left hand and then the legs. Yes, I am coming back to my senses. I was lying in the ICU and on ventilator support. Few pipes were coming out of my belly with a blood-like substance oozing out of them. The catheter was in place. Soon, a few doctors were there near my bed. From their discussion, I understood that everything had gone as per their plan and that I was recovering well. Suddenly, I noticed that the wall clock in front of me showed that it was 11:45 am. A lot of things started rolling in my head. I clearly remembered that I was in the operation theatre at 13:15 hours and, after that, I couldn't recall what had happened to me and now I was lying in the ICU bed with a heavy oxygen mask on my face.

After some time, my daughter came to see me and because of the oxygen mask, I could not talk to her. She seemed to be very scared, seeing all the paraphernalia attached to my body. My wife—I knew she couldn't withstand such a situation—so I signalled to my daughter to not send her inside. The visiting time was very limited, so my family waited outside and my son met me in the evening. Around eight pm, the senior doctors started coming again and removed the pipes from my stomach and instructed their subordinates to stitch the now open places. I felt better but drowsy all the time.

I was allowed some food in the evening. One more pack of blood was infused. My haemoglobin level was low. Suddenly, I heard the voice of the doctor—I could not open my eyes—but I heard him speaking loudly to someone in a very worried voice; he was asking them for some help from the cardiology department and the availability of the echo machine. In the evening, a few nurses came to me and fixed something in my chest area. I did not know what exactly that was. The cardiology doctor came and started doing my Echo. They were shouting as I understood over the phone to someone that the Mitral Valve that was replaced was not in place. They were contacting the Senior doctors who also rushed, and later, I understood from their discussion that the item put in my chest by the nurses was having some issue and so the Echo was coming out wrong. After correcting the same, the result came out to be okay. During all this time, I was in my full senses and was listening to everything fearfully but I could not open my eyes to see anything. Fear was running within me as I listened to their conversations. I was very worried and I felt that the doctor in charge of the ICU was very negligent. The work that was supposed to be done by him was given to the nurses. I did not want to be under his supervision. The morning when my surgeon and the doctor in charge came to speak to me, I told them what had happened the night before and requested them to shift me to the other ICU. They were very helpful and told me that they were aware of all that had happened to me and transferred me to the other ICU. Some disciplinary action was taken against the doctor in charge of the ICU that night, which I came to know later.

The other ICU was much better and the nurses and the doctors in their shifts were very cooperative. All the senior doctors were visiting one after the other, both in the morning and the evening and some tests would be recommended every time and all were saying that I was doing well. My family members were spending their time outside day and night. One person was allowed to visit me for only 15 minutes in the morning and another for 15 minutes in the evening. Seven days passed and I was shifted to a cabin where one of my family members was permitted to stay with me. After two days in the cabin, I was discharged but needed to come back for check-ups frequently during the next month. We took a furnished house on rent and stayed there for two months. In between, I had to be admitted twice after being required to report in emergencies. Anyway, after two months, I was quite well and the doctors permitted me to leave for home and report after three months for a check-up.

During the whole episode, I kept telling myself that everything would be alright since I never hurt anyone in my life intentionally and *Ma Durga,* who is my strength, would lead me to recovery. Anyways, what was going to happen, will happen. I had the best cardiologist and a full family supporting me, waiting outside in the central hall of the hospital half-sleeping in the chairs provided to them. During the days I was in the hospital, I left everything to God's will and in the hands of the doctors. I was mentally determined that I would be alright and that I have to be alright. During the entire process, I collapsed almost three or four times and the doctors were also worried about me and called my family to the ICU, which was normally not allowed unless there was an emergency.

A JOURNEY SET OUT

INITIAL DAYS AT SHILLONG

Someone from the control room in charge of the 132 KV substation was shouting for me, informing me that I had an urgent call from the State Load Dispatch Centre (SLDC), which controls the power flow to all the areas of the state and decides the import/export of power to/from the state. In other words, SLDC is the nerve centre of the state power supply activities. Engineers and support staff were placed on shift as it was a 24×7 activity. I was not allotted a quarter till then and I was travelling from Guwahati to Baihata Chariali. A restaurant with a very peculiar name existed there at that time. I used to have my lunch there and then take a bus to the nearest town from where I had to move to the substation. From the nearest town, my place of work was around seven to eight kilometres away. Jeeps and 407 buses that went to the substation area were always overcrowded and I never got a seat to sit down. By the time I reached there, it would normally be around noon and I had to return by 2.30 pm, which was when the last communication was available from my workplace to the nearest town, from where communication to Guwahati was available till night.

Even though the road from the substation to the town was only seven to eight kilometres, it always took nearly an hour as the road was in a very bad condition and the vehicle stopped nearly every minute to pick up passengers. There were only very few such small buses plying and the conductor never failed to pick up any passenger he found on the road as if there were never-ending spaces inside—people were just put inside the vehicle and practically there was no air or space to breathe. I, being a short man, sometimes found it difficult to breathe when I was surrounded by people taller than me.

I was with the Executive Engineer discussing a certain matter and he was very helpful and answered my questions always, even though sometimes I asked very silly questions. As that was my first job, I needed guidance. At that time, the in charge of the control room again shouted for me, informing me that the person on the call was waiting for me and had informed him that it was urgent. I was worried and ran to the control room to attend the call. I heard Pradip on the other end. We were classmates from our college days and had taken up jobs from the same organisation on the same day, but he was posted in the State load dispatch centre and was attending the shift duty there. He told me that our appointment letter had come from a central public sector company in the power sector with headquarters at Shillong, where we attended the interview a few months back and had practically forgotten about it before both of us were selected.

After some discussion about the future course of action, we found it better to go there immediately to understand the company and thus we travelled to Shillong the next day. For me, the actual aim was to just visit Shillong as it was one of the most beautiful places in the country and is called the Switzerland of the East. We met the officer of the HR recruitment section situated in the Dhankheti area in the centre of the town, which may be around five kilometres from the bus stop, on the fourth floor. There were very good local share taxi services available in Shillong. The officer in charge advised us to join immediately and told us about the benefits of joining the organisation. We were very impressed after talking to him and decided that it would be better for us to join a new organisation which was growing and was under the central government. We came back to Guwahati to submit our resignation as Assistant Engineers in our then-present company. I went to the 132kv Substation office the next day and the resignation process was completed. The Executive Engineer and my colleagues there gave me a very sentimental farewell. Within a very short period, I had become a part of the small family of the substation and although I decided to leave the job, I felt awful to leave my friends there. The team was so good and helpful.

After completing the resignation process, Pradip and I went to Shillong the very next day. Shillong is the nearest Hill station from Guwahati. It's a very beautiful place and the Barapani (Umium) lake welcomes you to the city. We went straight to the Dhankheti office to join the company and were advised to go to the office of the Additional Chief Engineer (E) at Motinagar to submit our joining report as he was the overall head of the Electrical/Mechanical wing. We complied and went there to complete our joining formalities. One Executive from HR, who was responsible for the guest house, arranged for our temporary accommodation and told us that enough warm clothes would be provided and we need not worry. There were no departmental quarters that came up then.

It was the month of December and at that time, Shillong was extremely cold and windy. We were provided with two light blankets in the guest house and the whole night, we were just shivering. In the office the next morning, we met our boss and came back to Guwahati to take our proper winter clothes and bedding. Our boss was a perfect gentleman and was maybe around 55 years old with a heavy build and was very polite and helpful. When we narrated the story of our first night there to him, he banged the HR guy over the telephone and advised us to get all our requirements, if needed from our home or to purchase them from Shillong. He also told us that he would give us a week to settle down and no specific work would be given for that period so that from the next week, we could fully devote ourselves to our job. He also indicated that no leave needed to be applied for this period, but thereafter, as a lot of work was going on in the corporation, we will not be allowed any leave unless it was an emergency. We left for Guwahati. The road from Shillong to Guwahati had a lot of turns, awkward gradients, and a single lane in some portions of the road and only expert drivers could drive those big buses there. Assam and Meghalaya State Transport corporation plied regular bus services between Guwahati and Shillong. After the bifurcation of Meghalaya from Assam, a lot of Assam government offices were still running from Shillong and were in the process of shifting. Most of the central government departments were in Shillong and, therefore, all buses were normally going full, especially on Fridays. Few tourist taxis were also plying, but we were yet to earn any salary. The previous job's salary was also not paid since we had left it in the middle of the month. Therefore, we avoided using taxis to control our expenditure.

We came back after two days with our required clothes to the guest house where our rooms were booked for a week. We started searching for a suitable house near our office in Motinagar or around the office and within a few days, we found a small house with two small rooms—one slightly bigger (we called it a hall later) with an attached bath and kitchen space. It was an old Assam-type house with a Hessian cloth ceiling at a very low level. Pradip was a tall person and the ceiling was slightly above his head level. But, during the cold, we found it was okay. It was very difficult to get a rented house in Shillong and we were elated to get a house near the office even though it was old and not in a good condition. We got water for one hour in the morning and evening as the water supply in Shillong was very bad (even now, it remains the same). With all those limitations, we were happy to get a house so easily and so quickly. We shifted to our house at the earliest. The problem started after shifting as we had no idea about cooking and also did not have anything like cooking gas, utensils, etc. We decided after a long discussion that we will try to do the cooking ourselves even though we had never done it before, which was indeed a very bold step for us. The owner of the house arranged for a maid for cleaning the utensils and the rooms for the coming months. Luckily, we got a gas supply connection without much effort through the help of one of our colleagues from Shillong and we brought some bare minimum utensils, which we felt may be necessary. We settled in our new place within a week. Pradip took the lead in the preparation of the meal as he had some better ideas than me. We had rice, dal, and omelette on the first night. I made the omelette reasonably well. We certified ourselves as good cooks and we declared to have a future in this field.

The first night, we enjoyed the self-made dinner and happily went to bed. Soon, I had fallen asleep. It must have been around six in the morning when I woke up and saw from my bed Pradip hanging himself from the ceiling upside down. I was terrified and called him loudly from my bed but there was no response. I was more scared even by the thought that he might have committed suicide and all bad things were coming to my head. With fear, I jumped out of my bed and came to him and shouted but still, my eyes were not fully open. Then, he laughed loudly and told me that he was doing *Shirsasan*. As he was a tall person, his legs were almost touching the ceiling. I shouted all the slang that came to my mouth and warned him that if in the future he wanted to do such adventures, he should give me prior notice.

It was extremely cold in the first week of January and the water froze. In the morning, we had to hammer the water tap a few times; otherwise, it would not flow. Bathing regularly was out of the question. We normally started preparing our food at night for the morning as well. In the morning, we got up quite late in the cold and were very scared to touch the water, so we used only hot water. There was no requirement for a fridge. In the mornings, we just warmed the food prepared the previous night, swallowed it down, and ran to the office that was only five minutes away from our house.

I was given a seat on the ground floor with my Senior, Mr. Barua. I was given the responsibility to look after the works of the Kopili Hydro Electric Project, where there was a major mishap two months back. I was to report directly to the Additional Chief Engineer who was the head of the Electrical/Mechanical department of the corporation without any officer in the middle as the Executive Engineer (EE) to whom I was supposed to report was on a long leave because of his medical issues. The next day, the EE who was heading the MRT (Meter Relay and Testing) Department came to my room. His office was also near our office. He was running the division alone with one JE at that time. He came to me, introduced himself, and told me to be ready by one pm as I had to accompany him to Kopili Power Station. I did not have any knowledge of the project and only knew that there was a major mishap in the tunnel system and the whole powerhouse was flooded and submerged with all equipment of the two machines that had been fully ready for commissioning. He came exactly on time on a red Gypsy. I sat at the back. It took around six hours to reach the Kopili power station and he instructed the driver to proceed straight to the control room, which was by then cleaned from the debris and the relays were kept open on the floor. The relays were of Electro-Mechanical type as Static relays were a later edition and were not available at that time. He immediately started working on the relays and asked me to keep the records. We were working and he was continuously smoking *Charminar*, the favourite brand of cigarette at that time, one after another. I was too hungry as I had taken my meal at nine am and only had a few cups of red tea here and there. It was about two am when he started to tire and he spoke to me, "Rajat," (he used to call me by my first name only), "Now we must go to the guest house and take our dinner." My hunger had already vanished by that time and the guest house was 24 km away. We reached the guest house at around three am. The road was called Surge Shaft road and both sides of the road were full of dense forests and had elephant herds crossing frequently. Food was kept in our guest house room but by that time, the food had frozen and could not be consumed. I took a hot water bath, felt relaxed, and slept without any food.

There was a knock on the door.

Either someone was at the door or I might be dreaming. Again, there was a knock.

I was in deep sleep and came out of the bed to open the door but forgot which side the door was. My eyes were still partially closed. I found to my utter surprise that it was the EE MRT at the door fully dressed and ready to move. Looking at me, he understood that I will take at least an hour to be ready. He left to the powerhouse alone, instructing someone to arrange a vehicle for me to come to the powerhouse.

I heaved a sigh of relief and went to my bed again. I slept one more hour nicely and had a heavy breakfast as I was sure lunch may not be in my luck today as well. By the time I reached the powerhouse, it was 9:30 am. The EE MRT had already completed the major part of the balance work and was smiling when I came in to apologise to him for being late. On the very first day of the project, I understood how people were getting themselves fully engaged in their duty and forgot everything except their work. I started enjoying it but was also scared but seeing the dedication of my superiors and juniors, I was immediately determined to be a part of the mission, which was "to restore Kopili powerhouse with full dedication." Some light lunch was arranged in a nearby house and we completed our job by eight pm. We reached back to the guest house within an hour. I was so tired but could not express it as the people working with me were older than me and they were all looking fresh. We came back in two different vehicles and I reached a bit later than the EE MRT. I found him and another officer I had not met so far having drinks in the portico of the guest house and the other gentleman was laughing at a full blast that I felt the doors and windows were also shaken by the sound of his laughter. Later, I came to know that he was the Senior EE who was in charge of the Khandong powerhouse where two units of 25 MW were commissioned in 1983. His laughter was his trademark and people used to know him for that! He was a very competent engineer and later I learned a lot about power systems from him.

Khandong was the first power station of the corporation in the Kopili river basin. The water of the Kopili river was stored in the Kopili reservoir by making the Khandong Dam and the water that came through the Khandong machines via Khandong Tail Pool got stored in the Umrong reservoir at a much lower elevation. There was a water conductor system (Tunnel) suitable for four machines of 50 MW each at Kopili power station and the first two were ready when the mishap took place. The second valve of the penstock II that was to be used for Units 3 and 4 was kept closed for the supply of water to the next two machines that would come in the second phase along with the second penstock. The work of the other two machines was not taken up and was planned to be taken up after the commissioning of the first two units. Similarly, there was provision for one more 25 MW unit at Khandong, which was to be started after the tunnel system was ready. Since I had not visited any hydropower station earlier, I was very inquisitive and asked all kinds of silly questions to whomever I met on my second day at the power station. Our dinner was ready and Baruah, the chief cook, called us for the dinner. The next day, we left for Shillong early in the morning. Luckily, Pradip kept something for my lunch and I went home and had it there. Whatever was there became so delicious for me as I was famished and could not have anything that early and the vehicle had not stopped anywhere on the road even for a cup of tea. I was in deep sleep after the food till Pradip came back from the office and woke me up. I now knew that I had to carry some food stuff while moving with officers like the EE MRT.

I slept the whole evening till Pradip came back from the office. We went out to the Laitumkhrah market near our house for some vegetables and to buy some fish. Since I used spectacles, the duty of frying fish was allotted to me. Pradip proved to be a much better cook, so I helped him with cleaning, boiling water and eggs, serving food, etc. Within a few days, we became reasonably good cooks and became capable of making food which we could eat without much problem. On the 31st of December, we were invited for an official get-together to celebrate the eve of the New year. All officers of Shillong from all the departments celebrated New Year's Eve at the guest house. All officers normally attended with some contributions, the HR officer who organised such events told us. We reached there at seven pm and by the time we reached the guest house, a few officers were already there. Drinks were in abundance and the officers were enjoying the same while playing engaging music. Snacks were served hot and since I had never touched alcohol before, I tried to avoid it by keeping busy distributing and taking only the snacks. The head of HR noticed that I was not touching the glasses, so he came to me. He was an ex-army officer in short service and had joined our corporation immediately after its formation in 1976. He was a tall and well-built figure and looked me straight in the eyes. I was worried. He approached me with a glass in his hand and very politely asked me to take the drink or otherwise it would be an insult to him on New Year's Eve. He then offered me the glass and prepared another for himself. I knew I was in trouble as he was standing behind watching me. I took my first sip. He was very happy and announced that he had made one more officer join his regiment. I finished the glass and found myself better in the chilly cold. I helped myself with a second peg without anyone forcing me. He was very happy but advised me not to take more. A fatherly figure respected by all and till his retirement, he treated us as brothers.

Three of us had joined the corporation at the same time and the third one was Mitu and she was from Shillong. Ashim Paul was seated next to her in a big hall on the second floor. Ashim had joined much earlier on a temporary basis and was later confirmed in the second list of appointments for our batch. We became friends immediately on the first meeting. She had joined a few days earlier than me and already had some idea about the office and the corporation, which she shared with us. She used to give us a lot of advice every day on the subject of preparing different food items but we had our doubts about whether she knew cooking as she was staying with her parents and her mummy used to pack her tiffin as well. We tried to do all kinds of experiments in our cooking, especially Pradip, who always came back from Guwahati with a new recipe.

After a fortnight, Pradip and I were sitting in Mitu's room having tea when a gentleman who was dressed properly came toward us.

"Please give me fifty rupees," he asked, looking at Mitu as she was facing him.

We had no idea about the person. I thought that Mitu must be knowing him. She with a surprised look on her face gave him the rupee and the gentleman vanished.

Then she asked us whether we knew him.

We said, "No!"

She told us she also did not know but had given the money as he was looking like a gentleman. We all were laughing about it. After half an hour, he came back and thanked Mitu for the help and introduced himself as Simanta, the newly selected Engineer of our batch. He did not have the change to pay for the cab, so he had needed the money.

We enjoyed the moment and later this topic also gave us a lot of entertainment. He also laughed about it, understanding his mistake in not introducing himself in the first place.

Tea was a must in Shillong and one Nepali gentleman, Sarmah, was providing red tea with some snacks he carried with him in a bamboo basket. A very cute child Mira, who was maybe around four or five years old, was his daughter and always came with him. He also put charcoal in a *Chulla* (fireplace) in all the rooms in the morning, without which survival would have been difficult. The heater was not used at that time in the office.

One Saturday, Simanta came to our house with a lovely girl with a round face. Since we did not have chairs except for the two chairs provided by the owner that we used as our dining chairs, we told them to sit on our bed. I hardly made my bed every day and so nobody ever sat on my bed. Pradip was very particular and kept his belongings neat and clean and, as a result, I used to regularly get some "sweet words" from him. Simanta requested that he also wanted to share our house if we agreed. We could not refuse his request as we had already become very good friends within the last few days. So, I shifted to the smaller room in the front and left the other big room (Hall, we called it) to Pradip and Simanta. The girl Gita, later we started to call her Mamu, which was her nickname, stayed in the North Eastern Hills University hostel and was a Ph.D. scholar and Simanta's fiancée. Soon, she also became a part of our group. Simanta was never available with us after office hours or on holidays as he was busy with his girlfriend. But I was happy that now the responsibility of our kitchen was taken care of by the three of us, the responsibility of cleaning the utensils and assisting Pradip was shared between Simanta and me as Pradip had already established himself as our chief chef. When Pradip was not there, Simanta and I were in great trouble to prepare our food.

Pradip was very particular about wrapping himself fully in his warm clothes properly while sleeping. First, he wrapped himself with an *Eri Sador*, a speciality of Assam, over it a blanket and then a quilt. His ears and head were covered by a muffler and so he always kept himself fully packed and slept looking at the ceiling. One night, he suddenly jumped from his bed and put on the lights, taking a stick in his hand and searching for something. I was observing him from my bed in the other room as we never closed the door in between. After some time, he went to bed again and slept. Simanta was not there that night and had gone on tour. The next day, I came to know that his nose, the only part coming out of his covering at night, was attacked by a rat. There were big-sized rats in our area that roamed around as soon as the lights were put off. The next day in the office, it was a hot topic and we all laughed at the matter! In our gossip even now, this incident comes up sometimes and gives us a lot of entertainment.

I went on leave for a week to meet my parents and Pradip was alone as Simanta was also on tour. He usually went to Guwahati on Friday evenings and came back on Mondays. I came back the next Sunday and was just opening the door when I smelled something.

But what was that smell?

A very foul smell was coming as soon as I opened the door and I shouted when Wati, my neighbour, came out of his house. He also could not enter as the smell was so bad. We called a sweeper who stayed nearby to find out the source of the foul smell.

Mr. Wati, my neighbour, was with me trying to help me. The sweeper, at last, found the source. Something was there over the Hessian cloth ceiling; it must have been heavy as the ceiling was drooping and the area was wet. We understood that something must have died there and we decided to cut open the ceiling. A cat was found dead and the smell was coming from it. The sweeper cleaned all those areas and I had to throw all my material that was on the bed. I decided to stay in the guest house that night and the next morning, I came back to my house and cleaned the space once again with the sweeper. The smell was gone. I had changed all my bedding. Pradip came the next day and laughed after hearing the story. He enjoyed it. There was something fishy going on, I thought. Later, we came to know that he was the culprit. Simanta and I were not there and as he was also going home for the next two days, he had put rat killing powder mixed with bread and placed it in the route of their movement to take revenge against their attack on his nose. Unfortunately, instead of the rat, the cat must have taken the same and died. I was in the mood to kill Pradip in anger after hearing that but could not do anything. Everyone was enjoying the story and that made me more and more angry. I asked him to pay me the cost of my new bedding, which he never did.

Days passed nicely and, on most days, I used to be in Kopili power station and on other days in Shillong as all the damaged material had to be arranged and I was the only person looking after all those activities from HQ and was required to report to Addl. CE (E) for Kopili restoration matters, which he reviewed every morning. Due to the absence of my Executive Engineer, I had to work late hours every day and reported directly to the big boss. A few months passed by and our Addl. CE was promoted as the CE (Transmission) and one senior officer from ASEB joined as the CE (Generation). Pradip and I joined the Generation project office, which was newly created. Mitu and Simanta remained under Transmission. As a result, both of us also remained with the generation shifted to the first floor and got a single-room chamber. I remained extremely busy all day and had to work on holidays as well and was required to travel to Kopili during odd hours. Within a short while, one Executive Engineer was posted in our office. DPD, we used to call him in short; he was quite a simple man but was a workaholic and unmarried. He must have been around 45 at that time but his joining had given me a lot of relief as a buffer zone was created and we could share the responsibilities. He was an excellent leader, colleague, and a very decisive person. He always asked us "to make decisions with fifty percent accuracy today rather than keeping it pending for a long while, expecting a hundred percent accuracy that is never possible." That learning was of great help for me in my latter service days.

The second list of our interview panel was out and Kamal and Amar joined our office. Kamal used to sit in my room and Amar in Pradip's room. Some other friends joined in transmission in MRT and Monitoring. One of them was NKM who was posted at the Doyang project directly. He was the only person posted on the project and was from the first list itself.

Gradually, we were settling down. I was the busiest person as the Kopili project had to be brought back and all efforts were made at all levels for early completion as per schedule. I was running between Shillong and Kopili very frequently. Telephone communication was quite deplorable in those days. Hundreds of items were to be ordered. The debris that needed to be cleaned by the site authorities, the damaged items that needed to be ordered for replacement, the contracts to be awarded for re-erections, and the insurance claims to be made were all managed by me and as I was very new to the work and procedures, it was a real hectic time.

After DPD joined, I was getting the much-needed support as earlier I could not talk to anyone about my difficulties other than with my CE, which was not always possible. Though I was extremely busy, I enjoyed every bit of what I was doing and was learning new things every day. My friend and senior, Srivastav, was in Kopili and Mr. Chakravorty, the OEM Engineer, was responsible for supervising the rectification works. We three very soon became close friends and enjoyed our work. When we came out of the powerhouse after working till late at night and travelled back in a Willys' jeep, the driver always knew what we needed after a day's long work. Having few pegs and singing without any knowledge of music. These noises relieved us from the tiredness of working the whole day and solving the problems, which included doing the crane operation as well if required. The surge shaft road, the shortest road to the guest house, would be in total silence as there was no traffic except for a few project vehicles and the sound of some insects that made the atmosphere frightening. A few times, we had to wait for hours when elephant herds were crossing the roads. They did not harm anyone but we were scared when we saw such big groups of elephants and remained seated in our jeep with its headlights on. We also noticed a lot of deer and sometimes wild pigs on the road during the daytime. One of our officers once reported to have seen a tiger on this road but we never met those.

Our head of Security sometimes came from Shillong with some sepoys and he used to hunt wild cocks. He always told us stories about his successful hunting but we never saw him coming to the guest house with his kills. We knew most of his stories were fabricated to impress us and we normally acted as if we took him seriously. One of my colleagues used to mimic him and made the caricature exactly in his voice word by word. Work, fun, serious discussion, enjoying the moonlit nights behind the reservoir with beer—all were happening simultaneously while we wholeheartedly put ourselves to our mission, which was the restoration of the submerged Units on time.

All our Seniors were guiding us just like our brothers and there was no junior/senior type of hierarchy. It was as if we were a family who only knew that the project was to be smoothly commissioned.

Sabir, who was the Assistant Engineer then and later became an Engineer in our panel, CS, and DG were the Junior Engineers and they took immense workload. I have noticed that generally, the people on the job need to be properly motivated to get the maximum out of them. They should be supported, giving more importance to motivating the team to get more involvement from them. Sometimes, a simple pat on the back does wonders and it need not necessarily be an award in the form of cash. People can do wonders, especially, if the employees feel their views are also taken care of without hurting their egos in the decision-making process.

Soon, the units were becoming ready. My stay in Kopili has become longer and longer. In the first quarter of 1988, the units were ready. The tunnel repairing work had also been completed and the pre-commissioning testing had started. After successful completion of commissioning tests, we decided to spin the machine. On the day the machine was put in the grid and given on load, many senior officers from the project and Head office were available. Unfortunately, there was severe vibration and the units needed to be stopped. After repeated alignment checks and balancing, the vibration was noted to be still beyond the permissible limit. The Kopili machines were the highest speed hydro machine of 600 rpm with thrust bearing at the top and the alignment of such machines was much more difficult than a bottom bracket machine. After a lot of research by the OEM designers and our team, the problem was finally diagnosed as cavitation. With some modification and after putting some predesigned fins and material below the runner, it was possible to break the cavitational chain. The machine ran perfectly well with the modification but we lost substantial time and revenue while finding out the solution and carrying out the modification. However, indirectly, it helped us to know more about the Francis machine's behaviour, particularly for me as I was a newcomer and I was able to fully involve myself during the entire process until the final diagnosis of the problem and the rectifications by even missing lunch or dinner on some days. Kamal and Amarjit (who recently joined in the Monitoring Department) also came on the commissioning day. There was great enjoyment and relief to all. Everyone's face had a glowing look and a special dinner was arranged by the then Superintending Engineer Hydro Generation Circle as designated on those days. CE (Design) who joined the corporation at that time was also there and we all drank and danced the whole night. The morning after breakfast, we left for Shillong with Kamal, Amarjit, and Ravi (who had newly joined as MRT Engineer) in a jeep with Rai as the driver. On the road, we stopped at so many places and finished a few bottles of beer. The corporation had earlier commissioned two machines of 25 MW of 300 rpm speed at Khandong and this achievement enhanced our capacity to 150 MW. There was bound to be enthusiasm among all the employees, especially the CEO, whose timely decisions and faith in his officers made it possible to restore both the units, including the water conductor system almost as per schedule. During that period, I found myself lucky to get the opportunity to be involved in such a massive time-bound job with a team so dedicatedly engrossed in their work. This was my first learning period as a field engineer and I took all the opportunity to learn from everyone, whether junior or senior, so that I could become an engineer in practice rather than an engineer with only a degree.

The next day, I rested for the whole day. Pradip and Simanta made the special dinner with mutton. After several whistles from the pressure cooker, the mutton did not cook properly and we had to put it again in the cooker. The pressure cooker's whistle was again blown several times but the mutton did not get tender and we could not consume a single piece. We had to take only the gravy which was quite good and kept the mutton in a bag for disposal. My neighbour Wati from Arunachal had a Labrador. The next morning, the dog was too happy to have all the mutton from the previous night.

Immediately after the commissioning of the Kopili powerhouse, the insurance claim settlement was a major job for me. The insurance company sent their surveyor Col. Kumar, a six-foot-tall, aged gentleman who enjoyed having tea very much. Our guest house was located in a beautiful location with the Umrong reservoir and had enough space in front with beautiful flowers planted meticulously by the gardener. At the front, there was a big open portico and Col. Kumar who was an early riser used to take a seat there after his morning walk and had his tea. When I came to join him, he would have finished a few cups already. Even then, I used to ask him if he would like some more tea and he always said, "Young man, I do not want a cup of tea. I need a couple of cups of tea." While working, he forgot everything and he did his job meticulously. I learned a lot from him during the process regarding insurance claim settlements. He also liked me a lot and treated me as his own son while teaching me all the intricacies and procedures. The claim was settled in full and the cheque was received. The Branch Manager came to me at Shillong with the cheque and I took him to our CE. All went to the CEO's room and he was sitting at the Dhankheti's office to hand over the cheque. Quite a memorable day that was! Col. Kumar was a respectable man and I regarded him as my father; he also enjoyed the silly questions I put to him and never got annoyed. My urge to learn compelled me to ask questions like a child, which paid the dividend in my later life.

***

"It is missing again," said Mitu, coming inside my chamber with a sad face. I was busy with something urgent. So, I asked her what was missing. She told me that like on the other days, some items from her tiffin box were missing.

She seemed to be suspecting me of it. But that day, I was so occupied with my work that I never went up to steal the tiffin from her room. I was laughing at her.

Now, she was confident that it was only me and left with a red face. That day, the culprit was Simanta. We all— whoever got a chance—stole her tiffin from her room when she was with her boss or was not in the room. Sometimes, it was me but I never kept her without her tiffin and we used to put something from Sarmah's basket. Her mother always gave her something special and as we all were missing that homemade stuff, we used to prank her. Later, she started bringing something for us as well so that her tiffin was intact in the box. We enjoyed doing this and she got a lot of importance and harassment from all of us, being the only female engineer in our group. She was very free and frank and took all the trouble without any offence. She also started creating trouble for us, too, so many times as a tit for tat. The tiffin lifter was always one of us but Simanta was the main culprit. Soon, Mitu's office was shifted to a room in front of KKC's room. KKC was the then SE transmission, a very serious and knowledgeable person. We all used to respect him but we were also terrified of him. However, outside the office, he was just like our elder brother. One day, to discuss a technical problem, I went to his room. He asked me to take a seat. I found him dictating to his steno as well as doing something in the files. Each work was going on simultaneously without a break. When he became free, he asked me what had happened. I informed him about the problem. To solve my problem, he asked me for a formula, which I did not remember. He deduced the same from the first principle and soon found the solution. I was so impressed. He was a mechanical Engineer but had so confidently solved a critical electrical problem, which we could not do even though we had come fresh out of college.

Barua was a very friendly guy and he always invited us to his house whenever his wife came to Shillong. Even if we did not get the invitation, we used to go to his house when Mrs. Barua came to Shillong. She was teaching Mathematics at a college in Guwahati and Barua stayed in Shillong and ran to Guwahati every Friday evening. Most of the officers kept their families at Guwahati and they left for the place on Friday and came back on Monday usually. We called them the Guwahati express. We used to eagerly wait for the day when Mrs. Barua would come as she prepared special dishes for which we longed. But suddenly, he resigned and joined a company in Guwahati.

My boss DPD was a workaholic. He used to mark all the files with comments like urgent/priority and immediately started following up on the intercom on the progress after sending them. We had repeated arguments on almost all official matters. He never kept his mouth shut and went on talking and making observations. In the evenings, he used to call us to his room to have a cup of tea together and all our anger would vanish. He was a leader who was admired by all his Juniors but he was a terror for his Seniors as he did not maintain any protocol and spoke whatever he felt was right. I decided that I would work with the files as per my assessment of priority as otherwise, not a single work would be completed in time with quality. I had the habit of going through something in detail before I wrote it in the file. At that time, computers were not there and all the tender documents were typed in stencil paper and, if required, corrected with a white-coloured fluid which was a very important item on the office consumable list. Nowadays, due to computers, all editing can be done in one place so easily. But in those days, we checked word by word, page by page, and made the corrections with the white fluid. Gradually, with computerisation in the Corporation from 1996, those requirements were over and people who joined after that period never saw Stencil papers, which automatically vanished from the consumables list.

To avoid preparing the general terms of the contract for each tender document every time, Mr. Halim from the Finance department and I jointly prepared a common general terms and conditions and printed huge quantities at a single time. It took away a big burden from us and only special terms and conditions of tender needed to be prepared against each tender if required. If different clauses were required for a particular tender in addition or at variance to the general terms and conditions, we only required to add special terms of the contract along with the general terms and conditions with a rider that if any clauses of general terms and conditions varied from special terms and condition, the latter would prevail. All our engineers benefitted from this act of ours and later this led to the development of a contract, 'Manual of the corporation.'

By that time, after having developed some knowledge of the machines, Erection and Testing and Contracts and Design, I was interested to go to a new project to lead the project team myself to get more confidence. Mrs. Rapthap was heading the office administration then. One very beautiful lady, Mahuwa, was working as the Lower Division Assistant under me. One day, I had given her some work and she made a mess out of everything. I was very angry as it was urgent and I scolded her. After some time, she came to my room—and unfortunately, Kamal was also on tour that day—and she started crying loudly. I was very worried and ran to Mrs. Rapthap's office, which was across from mine. She came and controlled the situation. I was in such an awkward position.

After Kamal joined, the atmosphere in my room changed and it became a concert hall after office hours. Everyone started coming to my room; Kamal used to sing very well and we had music sessions almost every day for an hour or so and felt relaxed after the office was closed. We were all bachelors then. The news reached the ears of the CE also, but he did not tell us anything—it must be that he was also like us during his youth. All our anxiety and stress from the whole day, we released during this one hour. Mitu had to miss our after-hour sessions as her father came to the office to pick her up. It was a big embarrassment for her then. In Laitumkhrah, we met Santosh da, a tailor with a small cloth store who was a friend of Kamal's. There was some vacant space on the side of his shop and that became our *adda* (gossip) place. It became a practice and any one of us coming to Laitumkhrah first reported at Santosh da's shop. He was a nice gentleman and helped us in many ways. Further, he was the contact point for us at Laitumkhrah and a treasure trove of information regarding all the beautiful girls of that area.

One evening, Simanta, Pradip, and I were gossiping about girlfriends while preparing our meal. We knew about Simanta's fiancée and so the attack was on Pradip. Others were confident that I was totally hopeless in this matter and left me alone. Pradip always refused about having one with a mischievous and shy smile, which was his trademark. After a lot of interrogation, he confessed that he just knew one girl who then studied at a college in Guwahati and that no further progress was there. The next morning, I was supposed to go to Guwahati for some official work and I jokingly told him that if he wanted to convey any message to her, I could help him. I was just teasing him then and went to bed. It was around 11 pm and I was almost asleep. Pradip came to my room and gave me an envelope to hand over to her. I jumped from the bed, woke up Simanta, and we enjoyed the episode in the middle of the night. Sometimes, we worried that the owner would throw us out because of the way we shouted and enjoyed ourselves at odd hours and while preparing our food that continued until we went to sleep. Our house owner was a very old man living with his wife, a married daughter, and his son; he was an Engineer working in some company in Assam and was not staying with them then. But no such thing happened. Aunty told us once that they liked our noises as otherwise, they would feel very lonely. We felt relaxed then and escaped from the big headache of worrying about being thrown out of the house. The next day, after completing my official duty, I went to the College girl's hostel to hand over the letter. I did not even remove my helmet because I did not know what the girl's reaction would be and I was prepared to run as well. That was also my first experience visiting a girl's hostel apart from meeting my sisters when they were in the University hostels. At the gate, I could not find the gatekeeper and was looking for him. At that time, a lady asked me who I was searching for and told me that she was the superintendent of the hostel. I became scared and lied to her spontaneously that I was looking for Mili and that I was a neighbour of hers. Her father had sent some money to give to her. The superintendent shouted to some girl and told her to send Mili, who was Pradip's girlfriend. Luckily, the superintendent left as she was in a hurry for something. I went to the visitor's room and sat in the extreme corner so that she wouldn't be able to see me directly. Suddenly, a girl who was quite tall and thin with long hair came to the gate and, not finding her guest, asked the gatekeeper who pointed me to her. Then she came and asked me whether I was Rajat da. I said "yes." I removed my helmet with relief as I understood that there would be no problem as she already knew my name, it meant that her relationship with Pradip was serious and that he frequently met her. He had the time to even tell her about us. At that time, only landline telephones were available and in the hostel, the instrument was normally in the superintendent's office; so, Pradip contacting her telephonically was out of the question. I had a nice time talking with her and then left. The next morning, I came back to the office and published the news widely to all our batch people and DPD. We had a lot of fun with the incident; I still remember the atmosphere on that day vividly. Pradip couldn't tell us lies henceforth.

Soon, our house became a place for *adda* (gossip) for all our bachelor friends on Saturdays if I were there. Pradip normally went on Friday evenings to Guwahati and Simanta used to be busy with his girlfriend. As the days passed, Saturday mehfil at our house became larger. Amarjit was a cleanliness maniac and he could not withstand dirt at all. My room was the place that irritated him the most. Whenever he came, he took the broom and went on cleaning my room before joining us. It was a great service I was getting from him, free of cost except for some "nice words" automatically coming out of his mouth. I waited for him so that the place would get cleaned. He was an astrologer cum palmist and everyone placed their hands to know their future, especially, about their marriages.

All came to our place on Saturdays with something to eat as they were aware that I was not going to prepare anything for them. We had a new friend Anil, who was an Engineer in MES. He arranged cartons of beer for us from the army canteen, which provided beer much cheaper than it was available at the marketplace. DPD was regular in his attendance. Our other colleagues had two more houses on rent, which we called Mess 2 and 3, ours being Mess 1. all came to our place on Saturdays. If I was not available on the Saturday, everyone got offended and asked DPD to not send me on tour on the weekend days. My other two messmates were normally not available on Saturdays. We played rummy and had beer from morning till evening and gossiped, sang, danced, and enjoyed ourselves. Though I did not know how to sing, I participated in all the activities. I assembled a tape recorder and there was no shortage of cassettes. Soon after the salary, I purchased a good player with a sound system to fill the gaps.

The new generation officers may not even see what a cassette was. How the tape of the cassette was rewound with the help of a pencil tip and played when the tape came out! Everyone used to come to my office room on Friday evenings to check whether I would be available on Saturday. One day, Pradip was also there and our party was also going on. Kamal was singing a melodious baul-geet after having a beer and then suddenly, there was a knock on the door. Pradip was a teetotaller at that time but he had joined us in taking the better part of the snacks. That day when there was a knock, he went to open the door thinking that someone from our group might be on the door. But he immediately closed the door after seeing the guest.

He came to the room where we were all sitting and playing rummy and having beer.

"Please hide all your glasses and put off your cigarettes," he said in a hurry.

We did not understand what had happened but looking at his serious face, we all obeyed him. All glasses were put under the bed and cigarettes were disposed of in the ashtray, which was removed. Everything was done very fast. Pradip then lit a few *dhoop* sticks in the room and again went to the door and allowed the guests to come inside. They were from his village. Pradip who did not take drinks would have had a reputation as a drunkard in his village, otherwise. He was very worried that the smell of the *dhoop* sticks would not cover up the smell of beer consumed by eight to nine people in a closed room. They stayed only for a few minutes and left after seeing the big gathering. They had also found themselves in an awkward position. When Pradip went to his house the next time, he was a very worried man, but after coming back he seemed to be happy and had his mischievous trademark smile back in his mouth and eyes. All of us were worried for him and felt relieved after seeing him come back with his smile. Those gentlemen had not reported anything in his house. Pradip's father, who was a teacher, was a very respectable personality in his village and if he had come to know that his son was drinking in our mess with such a gathering, he would have had the wrong idea. We were very relieved when he came back with a smile.

DPD was always behind Pradip and asked him to get married as soon as possible as he already had a girlfriend and a reasonably good job. He found Pradip could not concentrate on his work and that the work was suffering. We all backed DPD on this matter.

On Sundays, sometimes we—Pradip, Simanta, his fiancée Mamu, Mitu, and I—went out on outings with some packeted foods and enjoyed the whole day outside. The open space near the Elephant falls was our favourite destination. After Simanta's marriage, Mamu's mother also joined us a few times on our excursions.

MARRIAGE SESSION

"Pradip, tell me, what is your problem for delaying and not getting married?" DPD asked Pradip.

The trademark shy smile was on Pradip's face.

DPD persisted, "Tell me if there is any problem with the bride's house?"

Pradip smiled again without uttering a word.

DPD told him after having a few bottles of beer, "If there is any problem from the girl's family, tell me. I will make all arrangements to kidnap her and arrange your marriage at Guwahati court. No dearth of witnesses as we all will go and sign as witnesses. No need to hire an advocate also."

DPD had an LLB degree. Pradip was still laughing with his usual shyness. DPD sometimes forgot that he himself was unmarried, so we were also behind him, reminding him regularly to get married. He gave us long lectures on why he was avoiding marriage. He stayed near to our house and when he went to the Laitumkhrah bazaar on Sundays, I had to accompany him. He purchased very small quantities of fish but he would inspect the whole fish market. The fish sellers also knew him, but he did not care and went on from one fish seller to another, inspecting and bargaining. Later I used to leave him near the fish market and told him that I would be back within a few minutes to avoid him till he purchased the fish and came out of the market.

Every Saturday, he went to the Sani Mandir at the Police Bazar in the morning and took me with him. I had to get up early on a holiday, which was the most annoying part about going with him as I could not say no to him. After prayer, we used to go to "Kajol" restaurant to have our breakfast and then directly came to my house to join the gathering. He was also very careful in not spending his money and never took us to any good restaurant for lunch or dinner. But we all respected him and never considered him as our boss but as our friend and elder brother. Days were passing by very smoothly after the commissioning of Kopili as my workload had reduced substantially. Kopili Extension work was just at the preliminary stage. Pradip was looking after the works of Doyang HEP and he might have made a record of a sort by making the longest comparative statement with a lot of Easel paper (as at that time computer was not there), joining one after the other. Maybe, no one still has broken his record. Kamal was looking after Ranganadi HEP and Amar was taking care of the Assam gas-based project. All were in the initial phase and had not peaked up then. So, all of us did not have much pressure and only routine work was going on. Transmission project of Additional transmission line project connecting Khandong with Halflong in Assam, Jiribam in Manipur, Aiwal in Mizoram, and Kumarghat in Tripura was commissioned and design work of the 400 KV line from the AGB Project to Bongaigaon and Maldah was in progress. A Japanese firm was made as a consultant for the AGBP project and they occupied the ground floor.

As there was a shortage of experienced people and a few new projects were initiated, the management was contemplating the recruitment through the lateral entry and it was going on very secretly. Before the interview, we came to know about the recruitment process and all were very angry as this would hinder our promotional prospects. The people who joined in the first list of our batch and I were almost completing our qualifying requirements. We started protesting and met the CEO and all senior officials but even after all our efforts, seven people were selected; however, only three joined.

One day, DPD who was coming back from leave from Kolkata, his home town, called us all to his room and very proudly declared that he was going to marry soon. We were very inquisitive to know who the girl might be. He started by saying that she was from Kolkata and was from a very wealthy family and the only child of the family. He went on to say that this was his "last bus" but for her, this was "the last seat of the last bus," meaning that she was also quite late in getting married. Everyone laughed and congratulated him. Hearing our loud laughter, the CE also came to DPD's room and asked him what the matter was. He was also very happy and called Sarmah for tea and samosa. Soon, he married in Kolkata. After he came back with his wife, everyone, including the senior officers, was pressing very hard for a party. At last, DPD agreed for the same and gave all the responsibility to me and Manas, our friend who was in the Monitoring department, for a dinner at our guest house, which was at that time at Richa colony hilltop.

One Sunday morning, Pradip was in Shillong and we woke up early. It was in the month of March and the weather was quite pleasant. The sun was coming out nicely and we did not want to make our breakfast, so we went to Laitumkhrah to have our breakfast in Kajol, the restaurant where we used to take our evening snacks. There was one more restaurant opposite Kajol that came up around that time and was run by a few beautiful girls. After that restaurant opened, the customers in Kajol reduced and all were going to the other restaurant. We were no exceptions. However, on Sundays, it was closed, so we took puri-sabji at Kajol and decided to go for a walk. Shillong was such a beautiful place but we were always busy in our normal routine and hardly saw the places around except for our office and the Laitumkhrah market area from where we did our shopping. We took our groceries from a shop in front of our house owned by a boy of our age called Laskar. We reached Dhankheti and decided to go further as we did not know the areas in

Shillong. We were so involved in discussing some interesting topics, we did not realise it when we reached the road leading towards Cherrapunji. We crossed the Mahadev Than and Assam rifle camps and saw the signboard showing the road leading to the Shillong peak. We had heard so many beautiful descriptions of the peak and we felt it was the chance to see the peak. The weather was also quite good and there was practically no fog. We moved towards Shillong peak road. By that time, we were a bit tired as we must have walked more than 10 km already. But since we were so near, we did not want to go back. We rested in front of the Potato Research Institute for some time and started again but the peak was still far away. As it was Sunday, there were also very few taxis available and whatever was coming was coming with full passengers. Tourists from other parts of the country came to Shillong for sightseeing. We asked the people we met on the road how far the peak was and they didn't say much. We were going and going but not reaching our destination. The road was so beautiful and had greenery on both sides. After around seven to eight km of walking more, we reached the Air Force colonies where a signboard gave us the distance of another 800 m to the peak. We ultimately reached the Shillong peak and since it was a clear sunny day, we enjoyed the view of Shillong city, including the Barapani lake from the peak. It was such a magnificent view and even though we were too tired, we had to go back home and we did not have the energy to walk another 17 km. There were a few tea stalls, so we took tea with samosa and we slept there for an hour or so on a bench kept for the customers. We saw people going downhill through a small pathway running zigzag the way down. From some of the taxi drivers, we came to know that it was a shortcut road that would lead to Rilbong within 10-15 minutes. We got a solution to our problem and started going down the hill through the pathway. The gradient was too steep and going down was extremely difficult for us as we did not know how to walk down a hill and the whole pathway was filled with pine leaves making it very slippery. We walked for some time taking the support from the pine trees, later we took two pine sticks which helped us to walk down the slippery way. But somewhere, we made a mistake on our route and instead of reaching the road, we reached the backside of the residence of a Bengali family. We entered the house as there was no boundary fencing. One lady, most probably the house owner's wife, saw us and shouted something we did not understand. A gentleman came out and asked who we were. We told our story briefly to him and by this time, the whole family was surrounding us. They all were laughing after having heard about our adventure trip. By that time, we were offered tea, which we so badly needed. The owner left us on the road and luckily after walking around five minutes, we got a taxi to our house. We were not in a position to make lunch and instead took bread from Laskar's shop. With an omelette, we took the bread with butter and slept. Around 11 at night, I saw Pradip making something for dinner. I was also very hungry by then and came to help him. We simply made the easiest dish Kichidi and slept again after having our dinner. The next day, we had pain all over our bodies and it took nearly another two to three days to become fully normal. We decided not to take any such rash adventure in the future. But something else was in store for me in the later part of my life.

THE FIRST MARRIAGE PARTY

DPD had ultimately agreed to a party for his marriage and the entire responsibility was given to me and Manas, who was my friend and colleague. Accordingly, we arranged everything. All were asking whether sufficient drinks were available or not. Our priority was, therefore, to arrange the drinks from the army canteen through one of our security officers who was an army Major once. We brought two big turkeys, fish, and paneer for the vegetarians; a music system was arranged and all the officers along with their families were invited.

Some of the officers came straight from the office without going home and started the party sitting outside under the *Shamiana* erected for that day. The cook, Das, was making a variety of snacks and people started enjoying them. The family holders were coming a bit late. Mitu also came straight from the office and enjoyed the party. Suddenly, Das, the cook came to us terrified—his face looked as if he was about to cry. I asked him what the matter was and he told me that one of the turkeys that was kept outside for slicing was taken away by a dog. It was quite late and in Shillong, in that cold, getting a turkey was quite difficult. Manas and I immediately rushed to the market to find that all the shops were closed. Our driver Rem knew the house of one person who sold turkey. We went to his house, took him to his shop, bought a turkey, and then got back to the guest house. It was quite late and the CEO had started asking for dinner as he was used to having his early. Das had done a good job as he started preparing the available turkey without waiting for us.

We found that all our friends were almost fully drunk and only Manas and I were the exceptions. We felt pity for us as we were too busy with the arrangements. Ultimately, all senior officers and their families were served first, leaving the younger generation until Das made the second turkey that we bought late at night. DPD told the CEO that Manas and I were responsible for all the arrangements. The CEO knew me very well and he started to rag me.

"Why there is no sweet dish, Mr. Sarmah?" the CEO asked me.

"Sir, the party was to be arranged in a hurry and it escaped from our minds," I said, trying to cover up our mistake.

"Why was it arranged in a hurry?" he asked.

It spontaneously came to my mouth and I told him that the programme was supposed to be on Friday but as most of our officers go to Guwahati on Friday and as a lot of people did not take non-veg food on Thursday, the party had to be preponed to Wednesday suddenly.

The CEO was laughing out loud and joked that I should not make this type of mistake in project planning.

He was such a nice gentleman, one of the best Hydro Engineers in the country and was respected by all. Everyone was surprised that the CEO was talking to us for that long. He normally spoke very little. Manas and I straight away went to the other room and told our colleagues who were singing and dancing to supervise and we started our quota of drinks. Mitu was also a very good singer and even the non-singers performed very well as an accompaniment to the real singers. All were enjoying the party to the fullest, the juniors and seniors were all in different rooms of the guest house and the top management officials were sitting in the hall near to the fireplace. All had their dinner and most of the second batch people had hardly taken anything as their tummy was nearly full with snacks and liquids.

Mitu came to me after dinner and told me that my vehicle's driver Rem was fully drunk and she was scared to go with him alone to her house. Rem was earlier asked to drop her at her Kench's trace house, which was a bit far away. As she was so worried, I decided to go with her. I was fully drunk too by that time and had not taken my dinner but looking at the time and the grim look on her face, I decided to go with her and drop her off as there was no alternative vehicle available. When we reached her home, I saw from a distance that her father was waiting at the gate. It was around one o'clock. I told Rem to halt the vehicle at a safe distance and dropped her off without meeting her father. The next day, she told me that her father was angry as she was quite late but when she told the turkey story, the situation changed. The party was really good and all had enjoyed it. I was given unofficial leave the next day by DPD and I was so tired as well that I was not in a position to attend office. Ultimately, DPD got married even though it was delayed. Both the Last bus and the Last seat passenger on the last bus looked good and happy.

We think DPD was the one who opened the gate for marriage for our batch members. Mitu, who was a four feet 10-inch small structured girl with a lot of wit, presence of mind, and a very talkative nature, never told us that she was having a relationship. We had not even thought about that as she looked very young to be getting married and was a good friend to all of us; neither did any of us ever think she could also have a boyfriend nor did she tell us anything about it. Soon after DPD's marriage, she declared that she was also getting married by the end of January, which was only a few weeks ahead with her boyfriend from Tinsukia, who was a college mate of hers. Her family in the meantime shifted from Kench's trace to the Ram Krishna mission campus, which was very near to our office. Pradip and I were always asking her to give us a treat and ultimately, she called us to her house for lunch. It was a Sunday, so Simanta was busy with his girlfriend as usual. Mitu's mother was so nice but she could speak only Bangla and we two did not know Bangla. But we were going on talking with all kinds of Assamese-Bangla mixed up with each other and also with sign language and was communicating very well as Mitu also helped in translating when required. Lunch was served for all. Everything was very tasty but we found that all the items were dry and that dal or gravy was missing. I called her and told her in her ear to find some gravy so that we would have less difficulty eating as we normally took some dal type of liquid with either rice or chapati. She found some from the kerai with a lot of difficulty and gave it to us.

This made me recall an incident that happened between me and one of my friends a few years back. After the completion of our final year examination, we went to upper Assam cities like Naharkatia, Digboi, Duliajan Dibrugarh, etc. My friend's uncle's house was in Naharkatia and he was a very rich man who had a big business and a fleet of vehicles. He spared one along with a driver to us. We went to a place named Guijan where there were a few fish mahals leased by the forest department to the private contractor. My friend's father was a high official of the forest department and during his time, one Bengali contractor was allotted two such mahals and he was very grateful. Knowing we were in Naharkatia, he came to take us but we had tied up our programme for the next two days. We told him that we would come over to his house for lunch after two days. He was not very happy but understood our problem and told us that he will wait for us on the scheduled date. We reached there on time and Aunty (as we used to call the wife of the gentlemen) was so nice. It was a hot day and she came to us and used the bamboo-made hand fan for our comfort while she went on talking. She was so caring that we were scared that we should not make anything go wrong. After some time, we were called for lunch. There was no dining table as those were not common during that time and we all were sitting on the ground on a wooden "Pira," which is a small stool two inches in height. At that time, that was the normal practice in Assam. We found that there was a big brass plate in the centre where only rice was served and surrounding the main plate, there were around 10 small brass bowls, which were all filled with all kinds of delicacies; we did not know the names, but most of them were fish dishes made with different ingredients and different styles. In addition, there was mutton and chicken.

The head of the family, the uncle, told us to start eating. We started. I had something from the first bowl and water came out of my eyes as it was so hot and spicy. But the lady was behind us using her hand fan to keep us comfortable and kept asking us whether we were all liking the dishes and required anything more. I was in a big dilemma—if I left something on the plate, the lady would mind but she was so nice that we didn't want to hurt her feelings. She was treating us as if we were her children who had come home after a long time, so with all the punishment of hot chillies and pepper, I finished everything and told my friend that we needed to leave the place immediately as I needed to go to a pharmacy to get some medicine urgently. We left them after receiving all kinds of nice motherly advice from the lady. This incident will always remain in my heart.

***

Soon the marriage day of Mitu was approaching and they had taken a house on rent at Gora lane for that purpose. Mitu repeatedly asked us to help her family with the arrangements. She had an elder brother and a younger brother who was doing engineering. Once I visited his hostel in Bhopal REC when I was there for some official work at our OEM Bhopal. We visited her house one day ahead of the marriage and found that nothing was in order. When we asked her brother, he told us that everything was being arranged. But it was very late and nothing could be seen on the ground. We decided that if we remained as onlookers, there would be a problem and the elder brother would not be able to handle it. We got involved and went on working till the visitor's chairs were also placed. It was very cold outside in January. Luckily, Anil's Mess was nearby and we in batches went to his mess to have a few pegs and then came back. Nobody enquired whether we were taking any food even though Anil had arranged dinner for us at his mess. Mitu most probably noticed that and she came at around two o'clock with tea and some snacks but at that time, we were all in heaven and tea would not have served any purpose! It was almost early morning when we had finished all the arrangements for what we could do without any permission from the elder brother and we left for Anil's mess and slept there. There was no shortage of bedding material in Anil's mess and we were quite comfortable. We woke up at around 11 am and went to our house to have a bath and lunch as Anil had already left for his duty. We came late to the marriage location and found our seniors had also started coming. All our batch mates were sitting in a corner, gossiping. The groom and the party had reached the Shillong club and were camping there. Suddenly, we came to know that there was no vehicle being arranged for the groom to come. So immediately, I sent Harabhsan Singh, the driver of our CE's vehicle, which we were using for the last two days as he was in Delhi on tour. The groom reached and the marriage took place without any further problem. With a *topo* and a crown and in a heavy saree with a lot of decoration on the face, being a very short girl, Mitu did not look very impressive. One of us told the groom that he was supposed to propose to her but luckily, he did not. Laughter rolled all around and people were looking at us with curiosity.

We also enjoyed Simanta's marriage. He decided to have his marriage at *Ma Kamakhya Temple* at Guwahati. But till then, Mamu did not tell her mother. She had lost her father earlier. So, I had to take the responsibility of convincing Mamu's mother and I made her agree. Simanta had made all the arrangements with the Priest in *Ma Kamakhya*. We all came one day ahead to Guwahati and took a few rooms at Hotel Alankar in Chandmari. But unfortunately, a person of national importance died on the marriage day. All shops and transport were closed. We only had one jeep available with driver Rai. He was shuttling between the temple and the hotel. The marriage smoothly passed off and we came back to the hotel and enjoyed the evening, gossiping. The next day, we returned to Shillong. Simanta gave a party at Hotel Ambrosia at Laitumkhrah after some days. He had already shifted from our mess and had taken a house in Nongrim hills not far away from our mess. Another wicket had fallen. Utpal, an Engineer from MRT, joined in place of Simanta in our mess. Pradip remained the chief cook of the mess and every Monday, he tried a new dish he learned from his girlfriend. Once, he created havoc for us. He learnt a special dish with one particular leafy vegetable from his girlfriend and in the evening, after a lot of searching at Laitumkhrah, we got that vegetable and bought it. Pradip started preparing and while cutting the leaves, we found a very bad smell. But he, as per the instructions of his would-be, very seriously prepared the dish. Utpal and I were just looking at his preparation. We started eating our new dish that was called Masundory leaf with black pepper and it was supposed to be very good for the stomach. I just took the first gulp and ran to the washroom and started vomiting. It was of such a foul smell. Utpal and I prepared an omelette for us and never tasted that again. Pradip, I do not know how, had taken and finished his special Masundory dish taught by his girlfriend and smiled.

Sometime later, Pradip also got married to his girlfriend. As his marriage was performed in his village in Tihu, we, the full team, could not go but Utpal and I attended the same but came back early and could not attend the full marriage ceremony. As all the village seniors were present, we were also sitting there as decently as possible.

THE GRADUAL DISLOCATION OF THE SHILLONG TEAM

The promotion list of our first batch, Mitu, Simanta, Pradip, NKM, and I was out as Executive Engineers. Pradip was transferred to Ranganadi HEP in Arunachal Pradesh. Mitu also got herself transferred to Delhi on her request as her husband was working in Hindustan Copper and was posted in Khetri, which was not far from Delhi. Soon, Amar also got transferred to the Assam gas-based project and our group was breaking down gradually in Shillong. DPD was also transferred to Agartala and three new Superintending Engineers joined our office. I was given additional charge of Doyang HEP along with the Kopili Extension Project, which was becoming a priority by then and had to report to SE, BJ. Amar was also reporting to BJ till his release for the works of the Assam gas-based project at HQ.

At that time, another development was going on. The Government of India had decided to create an all-India organisation to look after the transmission system of the entire country and all central sector power corporations were required to hand over their transmission assets and manpower to the new corporation on an as-is basis. Of course, in our corporation, an option was given to the employees. Me, Pradip, Kamal, Amarjit, Mitu, Amar, and Jewel decided to be in the parent department and Simanta, Sisir, Paul,

Biman, and Utpal opted for Powergrid. We were sitting in the same building for some time; the first floor was for us, the same generation group and the ground floor and the second floor were occupied by Powergrid. Though we were in different organisations now, we were still closely connected to everyone.

The corporation had taken Kopili's Extension project on priority as all major works like the tunnel, dam, etc. were already completed before the commissioning of the first two units. I again got very busy as all the tenders of Kopili extensions were to be released after getting the specifications cleared from our technical consultant in Delhi. My visit to Delhi became frequent, which was very fruitful for me as it helped me to learn the design work of the hydropower station and my learning at Kopili's first two units became very helpful there. Most of our consultant designers had not much practical experience and depended on their strong theoretical knowledge. Combining field experience with their sound theoretical background made it easier for us to formulate the specification quickly and I soon had a few highly harmonious relationships with our consultants.

Doyang HEP, in Nagaland, which was started quite long back could not be started on the ground due to some local and insurgency-related issues and major works were not initiated. Only colony roads were started but there was trouble all the time and the engineers there faced a lot of difficulties. Around 1994, some agreement was arrived at by the central ministry with the state government and the local landowners and thereafter the main works packages were gradually awarded.

The groundwork of the Kopili's Extension Project had also started and I requested my CE for a transfer to that project as I had finalised all specifications of all 14 packages with our consultant. He always told me, "Okay, I will look into it and send you at an appropriate time." But one day, suddenly a junior officer was placed there as Construction in charge and I felt very bad. I conveyed my feeling to my CE and he also expressed his ignorance on the matter but he promised me that on awarding these 14 numbers of tender packages, I would be given the site posting. I have always felt that unless we work on projects and learn to manage them, we cannot become professional engineers. Assured by the CE, I was going ahead with the tenders so that I could move to the project at the earliest. That time, another issue made me very unhappy. Six lists came out for the training of our Engineers against our Assam Gas Based project and all of our batch people and Juniors were included for a month's long training in Japan with a substantial number of daily allowances in Dollars. But my name was never included in any of the lists. At that time, DKN assumed the charge of the CEO and KP was the Director Technical, which was a post created then. DKN was the first Director Technical and was one of the finest structural engineers in the country and after the retirement of the incumbent CEO, he had taken over as the CEO and Sri. KP joined as the Director (Tech). Also, a Director of Finance had just joined. Director (Tech) called me one day and told me that there was a mistake and my name would be included in the coming lists for training in Europe as the gas turbines were to be supplied by a European company for our Agartala plant even though I never raised this point as a grievance to any senior officers. Another six lists came out for the Europe tour soon but my name was never included. I did not approach anyone or complain even though I was very angry and hurt about the deletion of my name at the last minute. I was told that my name was always there in the draft order only to realise at the last moment that the same was deleted for whatever reason best known to the Management. I realised that only working would not do; we had to keep our bosses happy to get such opportunities. But I could not make myself convinced that, for a genuine matter, I should request someone in power. As the saying goes, "Desire dictates our priorities, priorities shape our choices, and our choices determine our actions." I, therefore, ignored such developments and as a result, I was never sent on any foreign training in my 36 years of service. I was the only person who was never sent to a foreign training programme when so many had taken place during the course of my long career. I did not think much about it. I kept concentrating on my job, which kept me always occupied and my urge to learn and experiment with new things made me motivated and I had already made a place of reckoning for myself in the corporation.

FIRST STEP IN FOREIGN SOIL

However, at last, God listened to my inner voice and I got a call for a Rockefeller foundation-sponsored global programme called LEAD (Leadership for Environment and Development) international fellowship. The selection test was rigorous and many IAS officials, Engineers, Media personnel, people from NGOs, and experienced personnel from varied fields were called for the test and group discussions held at India Habitat Centre, New Delhi. I came out successful and, in the evening, the list of the selected candidates was released. The interview started the same day. The panel consisted of very eminent personalities from retired Supreme Court judges and retired Secretaries to the various Central Ministries and people of learning in varied fields. I was a bit nervous but the members were so cordial and they tried to know what I knew and not the other way around—that is, how much I did not know—which was normally the trend in most of the Interviews. I was very happy with my performance but very worried too as the competition was among the best in their fields. When the selection panel was released, I was elated to see my name on the list of the selected candidates. Nine candidates altogether were selected and included; apart from me, one professor from IIT, one Engineer from a Maharatna CPSU, one IFS officer, one filmmaker, one HR head from Baroda, and three ladies— one CE from a state pollution control board, one senior professional from a Project construction CPSU, and one from Orissa representing an NGO—were there. I knew all the people by that time as we met during the period of wait for the interview. Within a few days, I got the official communication and the programme was for 52 weeks in total but not continuously. All expenditure for the programme was to be borne by the Rockefeller foundation but we had to send a no-objection certificate from the department, which would allow us to join the programme and state that our absence during the programme would be considered as on duty by the department. I had all the trouble in getting the certificate and I had to fight with the senior officers for the same. I was fighting because I knew I was selected on merit unlike the Japan-European team selection and it was my right to get the certificate as the corporation was supposed to bear no expenditure. In the meantime, I got communication, along with a personal letter addressed by name and signed by His excellency the President of Costa Rica, inviting me for a fortnight-long programme there. The outward and inward tickets were also received from the Rockefeller Foundation. However, I was yet to get my NOC to get my visa and also had to send it to the organiser to fulfil the requirement of documentation. At the last moment, I got the NOC and went to Delhi for my Visa. I reached the U.S. embassy at four in the morning as advised to me by someone who had gotten a U.S. visa earlier. But I was surprised to see the queue, which was already too long. At around six in the evening, I got my visa and with the presidential invite letter in hand, no questions were asked and I came back to our guest house in Delhi with the U.S. visa stamped on my passport. The caretaker of the guest house told me that my CE had been looking for me several times and instructed me to contact him as soon as I reached the guest house. I called him and to my utter dismay, he told me that I should not go ahead as per my programme and return to Shillong. I understood that there was some misunderstanding or someone was playing with me. I told him specifically that the question of my going back does not arise and instead, I would send my resignation by the next morning as I had my flight the next day night to New York. My CE understood my position and was satisfied with my clarification and told me not to make any hasty decision and that he would talk to the CEO and come back to me. After a very long hour of wait, finally, the phone rang and my CE was on the other side. He told me that he had a discussion with the CEO and I should go ahead as per my schedule. Though the problems were resolved, I was very angry about the harassment meted to me when I got an opportunity purely based on my merit. It made me more determined to perform and perform so that the people who were playing with me would automatically understand how difficult it would be to touch me. I told the guest house boy to get me a drink from the nearby wine shop and after taking a few pegs and a hot bath, I got relaxed. I decided not to think about it and concentrated on my preparation for the next day. The programme was so successful and taught me very important lessons, the first one being "a decision should not be taken looking only from one's own perspective but also the perspective of others." That was why people were selected from varied fields and so many countries. We were given teamwork and always the teams were changed to mix up members from different countries and different professions. Every evening, we had to present the findings that were to be moderated by experts. My first presentation was horrible as I had never had the experience of public speaking. I told my roommate Bijay, an IFS officer (we were given a room on twin sharing basis) my problem. He advised me to go to the bar before the public speaking and his advice clicked. My next presentation was really good as my friends were telling me later. On the last day, his excellency the President of Costa Rica was with us for the whole day and in the evening, the certificates were given to us by the ex-Commonwealth Secretary-General, Sir Sridath Ramfall, with his signature on it. We were virtually crying as we got separated after a fortnight's stay and had to leave for our own countries the next day. We made so many friends, interacted, enjoyed, and had food together in an open buffet with a grand musical night on the last day. Our ladies made the ladies from Canada and U.K. wear sarees and some of us were wearing the Nigerian dress on the last day of the programme. It was such fun and learning together.

The total 52 weeks of the programme were designed in such a way that was bifurcated into the national and international programmes. All the programmes were for a maximum period of two weeks, each for a total of 52 weeks in the next three years and we got the fellowship certificates after the completion of that period. I consider it a great honour and recognition. The other international programmes were in Zimbabwe and Chiangmai in Thailand.

One day during the Zimbabwe programme, around 70 of us decided to go see the Victoria Falls and took the flight from Harare. The programme was made through a travel agent with our own money as it was not a part of the course. Few buses were waiting for us at the arrival to take us to the fall. The water jets were coming to us from a long distance before we reached the fall and we had to hire raincoats, which were available on rent. We enjoyed ourselves so much that we forgot that we had to catch the return flight and the drivers of the buses were shouting at us. Anyways, one or two of us were missing. Ultimately, we reached the airport and were delayed by 45 minutes. When we reached the airport, the flight was already taxing in the runway after waiting for the 70 missing passengers for a long time. We were running to the counter and since there were nearly 70 people, the airport authority was kind enough to halt the flight from take-off to accommodate us. If we were late by another five minutes, we would have missed it and would have had to stay at the airport only as there were no more flights available that day. I still remember the beauty of the falls and the Baobab tree, which was supposed to be very old and had covered a vast area.

In Chiangmai, when the programme was at the Chiangmai university campus, we had a problem with one of our Indian friends as she was a total vegetarian and did not even take an onion. But in their preparation, even in rice, they put the egg. This created a big problem as she could not eat any of their food. One of our teammates was a Punjabi lady and she found a Gurudwara nearby and we all started taking our lunch in the Gurdwara langar. In the evenings, we went to the market not far away and found a lot of Indian restaurants. Dance and songs and other live programmes were going on till late every night at the centre stage and people enjoyed the musical programme while having their food. We were losing our official dinner arranged by the organiser for the sake of our lady friend from UP.

Finally, after completing the 52 weeks of training, which was based on a very different concept, we got our fellowship certificate. It was a great experience for all of us and it helped me to be more mature in decision-making in my later career. It made me realise that life is a journey with problems to solve and lessons to learn but, most importantly, with experiences to enjoy.

LIFE IS CHANGING

After Simanta's marriage, they started staying in a different house in Nongrims hills. Pradip also shifted to the project. Utpal and I were the members of our famous mess as we had decided not to take any more people into our mess. The evening mehfil and Saturday get-togethers were gradually over. One evening, Utpal and I visited Simanta after office hours. We heard a loud laughter from the house and knew that someone else was there. He was having some guests in his house. Hesitatingly, we entered the house. We found two very beautiful girls, whom we later came to know as their family friends visiting from Guwahati and a lot of fun was going on. Soon, we also joined them. The elder one was quite beautiful and impressive and Mamu was noticing my interest in her activities. She said loudly, "Rajat da, forget about it, she is already engaged with one of her classmates from Guwahati medical college." I scolded her from the outside but internally felt very bad. The ambience was so good and we all enjoyed it and we came back after having dinner at their house. Her sister was studying in college and sang very well but was much smaller than us in age even though Simanta was hinting at me to try for the younger. Utpal was also a very good singer. That was a great evening and we didn't have to make dinner, which was another relief for us.

Many small incidents in life taught us a lot in life. I remember when BG, our CE, was calling for the peon around 5 o'clock but no one reported even after he pressed his bell many times. Very annoyed, he came out of his room to Mrs. Rapthap's room, who was the administrative head of our office and found that she had already left. He was very angry. We never saw him angry and he always had a smiling face even during critical arguments. The next day, we found him near the staircase with his Pipe. He was a chain smoker and the pipe was his trademark and all the employees had to cross him to enter the office. Similarly, in the evening he did the same. This was going on for a few days. He scolded no one or issued any advisories. Within a few days, the attendance in the office was 100 percent and nobody left the office till the boss left. I learnt a great lesson about man-management without even speaking a single word and how to maintain discipline. That was a great innovation on his part. Now, many organisations have a biometric attendance system or face detection system. I was not in favour of such things from the very beginning, as after having all the technology linked with pay, employees come and go on time for their salary mechanically but their output has reduced because they are not motivated or guided and the management cannot give them sufficient work, at least to keep them busy for the day, or give them the due recognition without bias. Sometimes, the best performers were given excessive work that was beyond their tolerance and got demotivated while others were not given sufficient work assuming them to be non-performers, which made the latter demotivated. Knowing how to distribute work among employees is an art required to motivate them and only very few people develop such qualities in them. My experience with foreign training in my company was one of the demotivating factors but my hunger for learning has kept me going without it affecting my performance. Rather it helped me to perform much better. My father taught me one lesson from *Bhagwat Gita*: what is destined will happen and we the people or nature are only the means through which "God's will" is implemented. So, it is important not to have a bad feeling attached to the people who harm you as they are not the ones who do it but they only act as per the will of God. Even then, one feels bad when they come to know that someone was trying to harm them.

Our CE, BG, resigned as he was not considered for the Director's post and when he was the most eligible candidate as per our view at that time. He joined as Member Technical of a State Electricity Board and the CE Design temporarily took charge of our office. Later on, BN joined as our CE.

TYING THE KNOT

I was also under pressure from my family to get married and they were busy finding a suitable match. One day, I got a letter from my father as during that time letters were the only means of communication and very few people had residential telephones. He informed me that he had visited a family in Jorhat and their younger daughter was of his choice. He advised me to make a visit to their place at the earliest. Utpal had a plan to go to Dimapur substation and with him, I went to Golaghat. He left for Dimapur then and the day after he came back from Dimapur, we two visited the family and met the girl whom I found to be quite good and as a good match for me. Further, as my father had already visited them, I did not want to go another way without any reason. We soon got married. Amarjit and Utpal were there and Aravinda and Jewel, even though they started on time, reached one day late for the marriage. One of the most memorable moments in my marriage was when I got a telegram from my CE in charge at that time, wishing me all the best. It was special because before leaving for my house, I had invited all my friends and colleagues personally. That time, the CE was in Delhi on tour. I tried to contact him over the telephone so many times but was unable to do so. I kept an invitation card on his table and then left. On the day of the marriage, I was so surprised and happy to get a telegram from him, wishing me all the best. I treat this as a treasure and blessing and have kept the message still with me. That time, telegram was the only means of the fastest communication along with telex and later Fax machine started. In our corporation, for official internal communication, we used wireless transmissions, so all locations which had wireless facilities were manned by the security department. The marriage passed off without any hitch. I came back to Shillong and started searching for a house to bring my wife as the existing house, even though it was found convenient for bachelors, was not suitable for a family. After a long search, I could not arrange a house. One day, Ravi my colleague told me that the ground floor of his rented house was vacant and that I could take that. I went to his house in Rilbong and found the house good enough but quite far from my office. Transportation wise also it was inconvenient as I had no car or bike with me at that time. There was no alternative until I got a house near the office, so I took the house temporarily and brought my family to be with me in Shillong. My life had changed. Luckily for me, my friend Paul's house was just 100 m away and my colleague, Ashis, who had also recently married took a house nearby. Ashis and I went together to the office and both the ladies used to schedule their programmes together for the day. There was another part on the ground floor where a gentleman named Das was staying. His wife was also new to Shillong. My wife did not know Bangla and Mrs. Das didn't know any language other than Bangla. But they went on talking for hours together with each other; it is still a mystery to me how they actually understood each other.

While I was in Rilbong, once my family was with my parents after my daughter was born. One night, I got a pain in my belly almost after one pm. The pain gradually increased and I was very uncomfortable. I took a few painkillers but I did not get any relief. I repeatedly had to go to the washroom and was running from one place to another. It gradually became unbearable. I was waiting for the morning but around four am, I could not control myself and went to Ashis's house and called him. He was terrified seeing my face at that odd hour. I told him my problem. He knew a senior doctor and went to his house in the early morning itself and the doctor prescribed one medicine and asked me to go for a sonography. The medicine helped me and I left for Guwahati for the sonography as it was not available at Shillong then. It was diagnosed with multiple kidney stones. The doctor advised me for an operation. I was very scared of any operation of any sort and that was the reason I did not appear for the written test for the medical college admission, even after filling up the forms and getting admit card on time. I needed someone from my family with me during the process. I went home. While going to my place by bus, my co-passenger told me that he had a similar problem a few years back and took homoeopathy medicine from a particular doctor. He had given me the address and told me that the doctor had cured him and no operation was needed. I thought, what would be the harm in giving it a try if with that I could avoid the surgery. I went to him the next day. The doctor after looking at the sonography report told me that it can be cured but I should have patience for 45 days. I agreed. After around 20-25 days, I felt that the stone was going out with my urine and there was minor bleeding as well. I took another sonography, which confirmed that the same was no more there. What a relief! But as advised, I continued the medicine for one more month to be rest assured that it is fully gone. The pain was so horrible. Ashis, my friend, who was of a very jolly character, imitated my condition on that day sometimes when we met.

CHANGE OF BOSS

After the resignation of BG, DS was our CE for some time with dual charge till BN joined as our CE. He was a very talented engineer and his academic records were exceptionally brilliant. He treated us as his brothers and tried to explain the things we were not comfortable with. One day, he gave me a file and asked me to take the file home and study it properly and put up a draft and not to write in the file before he saw the draft. I took the file and after reading it once, I found nothing critical and hence wrote the draft. The next day he called me and asked whether I read the file properly. I told him yes and gave him the draft. Without going through the draft, he asked me whether I have considered a certain matter or not. I understood my fault immediately and grabbed the file from him and came back to my room. He was laughing. He gave the file to me in order to test me it seemed and I failed miserably.

The Boss and our consultant were very friendly and BN had a reputation and all the consultant officials respected him. During any matter that was not resolved at our level, the issues were escalated to him and the top-most level of the consultant. In such meetings, he always took us along and allowed us to go on arguing with the consultant or even with the Director and never spoke a word but watched us argue and counter. Then all of a sudden, he would start talking, "From what I understand from your discussion..." then he would dictate the decisions to the steno for the Minutes. Later, we understood that the decisions were taken by him before coming to the meeting and he allowed us to argue so that our egos were not hurt and consensus decisions were taken as an outcome of our discussions. We became more and more mature and diplomatic in our dealing with others, looking at the strategy of those brilliant people who had taught us by example.

After the start of the Kopili Extension Project, I requested my CE to place me there but a much junior person was placed instead of me. I was very offended and argued with my CE. He told me that he will put me on site as soon as the Kopili Extension tenders were awarded as all those works were handled by me. Apurba was a newly joined engineer attached with me who was a very serious Engineer and I was getting support from him. Things were progressing well.

I also got a house in Motinagar soon and shifted there. In the meantime, in 1994, my transfer order to Doyang HEP was out. Due to the very bad law and order situation, no one wanted to go there, so the management had selected me anticipating that I would also not be ready to go there. But I considered this as an opportunity for me to perform independently and to prove my critics wrong. However, BN did not release me till all the tenders were awarded. I shifted my family to my hometown and shifted all household materials except a bed and a few kitchen items. At that time, I had to leave for Costa Rica as a part of the Rockefeller training programme. After coming back, I fully got involved to complete the tendering or awarding processes and told the CE to release me. Ultimately, after more than a year of my order, I was released and I moved to Doyang hydro Electric Project in December 95'.

After coming to Motinagar, I got a very good neighbour who was a professor at St. Anthonies college, one of the oldest and most reputed colleges in Eastern India and his elder sister was a Senior officer at the Botanical Survey of India. Manas was my close friend and his wife was also from my home town, so I normally dropped my wife at Manas' place with my baby girl. Manas' mother was like her own grandmother and both the families were very close.

While in Shillong, Pradip was looking after the Doyang project and his first tender was for the procurement of DG sets with associated distribution systems for the construction power and colony supply. DPD was making a lot of fun about the comparative statement he made which was most probably the longest CS ever made. Even now, when we go through any CS, we always remember Pradip's CS and that none could so far break his record.

Powergrid's office soon shifted to the old Arunachal secretariat building, which was quite far from our office and gradually we lost contact with our friends who opted for Powergrid. After the shift of our friends to Powergrid and their transfer to different locations, our group gatherings suddenly got limited. Most of them had a family now and evening musical sessions automatically stopped one day. Mobile was a present-day addition and at that time, only limited landline facilities were available and it was normally provided from the superintending Engineers' level only.

After more than a year of my transfer order, finally, I got my release order from the Shillong Generation office to Doyang HEP as Executive Engineer and in charge of all Electro-Mechanical packages of Doyang HEP. I moved there soon.

DAYS IN DOYANG HYDRO ELECTRIC PROJECT

MOVING TO THE PROJECT

All of a sudden, there was chaos all over and everyone on the road started calling out, "It's going down, it's going down." It was a terrifying moment. I, along with my fellow workers, started hurling stones at the 42-wheeler trailer that had started moving downhill, carrying over 30 tonnes of over-dimensioned consignment. After an intense period of 5-10 minutes, the trailer finally came to a standstill. It stopped just half a metre from hitting the hill at the back, after having burst almost half of its tyres. It was a sigh of relief. That was in the first quarter of 1996 when I joined as the 'in-charge of Electro-mechanical works' of a Hydro Electric Project in the Wokha district of Nagaland. The road conditions there were extremely poor with dangerous curves and gradients along the foothills of Merapani. The foothills were around 10 km from Merapani along the borders of Nagaland and Assam. These made the transportation of heavy consignments extremely difficult.

I still remember the day—I was travelling from Golaghat (my hometown in Assam) to Doyang HEP by road, which was at a distance of around 70 km. It took me nearly five hours to cover that distance due to the deplorable road conditions. Back then, I travelled by a wide-bodied Jeep, which was the official vehicle for me for some time, but soon it was declared unusable. That day, my journey started in the early hours of a sunny December morning in 1995. Mr. Nath was the driver of the vehicle. The jeep was fully packed with food items, including live poultry and four or five co-passengers who worked in Doyang HEP whom I had met for the first time.

The road from Golaghat to Merapani was pretty decent till Furkating, a railway junction in the Golaghat district. However, after crossing Furkating, the road conditions started getting worse with various rough patches in between. Once we reached Merapani, Nath stopped the vehicle in front of a tea stall for a quick snack. I later realised that the stall was the unofficial eating spot for the DHEP project professionals and every project vehicle would halt there for people to grab a cup of hot tea, parathas and jalebis, which were popular among everyone. That tea stall was the only eatery available till one reached the project complex. The owner of the stall was a middle-aged Marwari gentleman, Mr. Sharma, who could speak fluent Assamese and ran the stall along with his son. Marwaris have a huge presence in Assam, with most of the trading and businesses run by them. Once we devoured our parathas and tea, we had some paan and got back on our journey. A few kilometres from the eating joint, our vehicle was stopped at the CRPF checkpoint to look for any untoward entry into the Nagaland border. The driver got down, made some entries for our vehicle, and the bamboo barrier was lifted shortly.

Within a few minutes, we reached the Merapani foothills of Nagaland. The road further ahead was in a pathetic condition with a lot of unscientific curves and gradients. As we went uphill towards Bhandari, a small village in the Wokha district of Nagaland, we saw a lot of children on the road running toward our vehicle. I was clueless as to what could be the reason when Nath explained to me that as only a few vehicles, and that too mostly from our project ply on that road, vehicles in general have become the new thing of interest for these children. Seeing the excitement in the eyes of those children, I remembered my school days when I first saw a helicopter land in our small town when the whole town gathered to see the "special bird," which they called it then. While I was engrossed in that thought, in an instant, while the vehicle was plying at a slow speed, two youngsters jumped into the back of the jeep as another stepped on the spare wheels at the back, holding on to one of the handles for support. I was shocked to see what had just happened but again Nath told me that these are routine events here as there were no other means of transport and communication in the area. Native people of the area used to walk long distances carrying goods with them and when they get an opportunity to ride on a vehicle like ours, they would never miss that chance. To break the monotony, I started talking with one of them in broken Nagamese. While I did not know about the language much then, I became fluent in it after being posted in Nagaland for six years. After a few kilometres of the bumpy ride, our vehicle was stopped again at a checkpoint after which there was practically no road ahead. It was mostly dusty and muddy lanes with ponds all along the route. We were impatiently moving ahead to reach our final destination, DHEP.

After Bhandari, we reached Bagti, a small hamlet of a few houses where I was delighted to see the signboard of a Bank branch hanging onto one of the houses. I was happy to realise that some banks have penetrated quite deep into the inaccessible areas and provided services to the people. While waiting impatiently to reach our destination, we realised how we all were covered in dust, giving us a very tired and rusty look on our faces. I kept bothering our driver Nath after every 5-10 minutes asking him how far we are from reaching our project. Each time he responded with a smile, noticing my eagerness to reach the site. On the way, Nath stopped our vehicle at some fixed locations, for everyone to attend to nature's call. From Bagti, we reached another small hamlet called Sanis, after which the road took a 90-degree turn. The route afterwards was narrow and had a lot of curves in a downward gradient and we started moving downhill. Nath pointed out with his finger the project location from there, which took us another hour to reach through the Doyang Bridge that was made long back over the river Doyang. We passed through another checkpoint but unlike the previous ones, there was no requirement for any registration or other formalities. The bamboo barrier was lifted immediately and a security guard welcomed us with a salute.

I was extremely content to see the project guest house after five long hours of a tiring journey with all of us and our belongings covered in dust. The caretaker of the guest house welcomed me with a smile and showed me my room. He mentioned that as the water connection work has not been completed, my washroom was not connected to a direct water source. Hearing this, I asked him to provide me with water in buckets as I needed to take a bath after the ride. He readily agreed. After the refreshing bath, I realised how hungry I was and went to the dining hall to look for food. I was served a plate of rice, a few chapattis, some plain dal, and salad to go along with it. While the food was simple, the journey and the hunger made it taste so delicious in my mouth. After the scrumptious meal, I headed to take a short nap. But alas! I was called in by a security guard to meet the Chief Engineer of the project, BB, who wanted to see me in his office, which was a three-minute walk from the guest house. BB had a very gracious and pleasant personality. In the first meeting itself, I realised the great opportunity I have got to be able to work under such a dedicated senior officer. BB welcomed me into his office, where other senior officers of the project were present as well. He welcomed me and explained to me in detail about the current situation of the project and what was expected of me while we sipped on some tea. All the senior officers were quite amiable and welcomed me to be a part of the team. This happy welcoming made me forget about the exhausting journey I had taken a while ago. During the informal meeting, BB mentioned that I should be required to meet with the Resident Chief Executive of the project (RCE) who happened to be a very strict administrator and disciplinarian. He always abided by time strictly, and even if a person got late by five minutes, there were instances of him cancelling their appointments. Listening to this, I made a call from BB's office to the office secretary of the Resident Chief Executive over the intercom. I felt fortunate to get an appointment scheduled for the next day at nine am. After the meeting, I walked with a calm mind to my room at the guest house and instantly went to bed to take some rest. I woke up when a boy named Dhiren knocked at my door and called me for dinner. I had a quick dinner and came back to my room and again went straight to bed thinking about tomorrow's meeting with the RCE and soon fell asleep.

We were just going on talking and talking. Of course, I need not have to talk, only listen and listen. The beautiful lady with me went on speaking nonstop. Then we went on a long drive, maybe near the road beside the sea and after a long hug, I dropped her at her house. She was about to kiss me but suddenly...

Cling, cling, cling.

The alarm clock rang in its cruellest sound indeed. Why this always happens to me, I do not know.

Seeing the clock, I jumped out of the bed in a panic, it was eight am already.

MEETING WITH THE RCE

It was 8:45 am sharp when I reached the RCE's office cum residence. I was tense as I had heard so many terrifying things about him and regarding his knack for discipline, punctuality, and professionalism. I met his PS and came to know that he had gone on his regular site visit to various work fronts and was expected any time. I was offered a seat and then only I realised that I had forgotten about my breakfast to catch up with the scheduled time. I was looking constantly at my watch and expecting him at any time with fear in my heart. Exactly at two minutes to nine am, the intercom of the PS rang and he handed the phone to me. Terrified, I took the phone with a trembling hand and heard a clear metallic voice from the other side.

"Am I talking to Mr. Sarmah?"

I said, "Yes, sir."

"If you do not mind, can you wait a few minutes for me as I am stuck up with some issues but shall reach the office within 15 minutes?"

I told him that since it was my first day at the project, I had no specific engagement and shall wait. He laughed and dropped the phone. I was so impressed by his decency and his faith in punctuality.

Exactly at 9:15 am, a white Gypsy stopped at the gate and everyone stood up to attention. I understood that the Boss had arrived. I saw a gentleman with a medium build who had a white t-shirt and a brown jacket on with sports shoes and a Mexican cap coming towards the office and asking his PS about me. Seeing me, he welcomed me with a handshake and ordered me to his room. I followed.

He was talking to me in his heavy voice. His eyes constantly gazed at me. I understood that he had all my background checked already and seemed to be very satisfied. I was the first electrical man after he joined the project. The RCE had retired as the Chief Engineer of Nagaland Electricity Department and our CEO had requested him to be with us on contract for the smooth run of the project as an experienced person from Nagaland. He called me to the next room, his dining room. The cook had already made breakfast for the two of us. I was also very hungry and finished all that was on my plate. He told me that he had full faith in me and that I would be able to complete the powerhouse work on time. I thanked him for the encouragement and left his place. All my fear had evaporated. He was such a gentleman, a fatherly figure, and a straight-talking person. I was too happy.

I came to my SE's office to submit my joining report. One young lady office assistant and another office attendant sat in the front room and the SE sat in the adjacent room. There was one more room for the draughtsman. Ms. Jeshubeni, the office assistant, had not known me earlier and she asked for my particulars before allowing me to be in the SE's room. I was impressed with the way she handled her work. I entered the SE's room and seeing me, he got up from his chair and welcomed me.

I saw a lot of electronic items lying on his desk and he seemed to be busy with those items doing some R&D. I submitted my joining report. He asked me about my meeting with the RCE and I briefed him only to his utter surprise that I had breakfast with the RCE on the very first day. He told me that I was very lucky as the RCE normally did not entertain anyone.

He seemed to be a man more interested in his hobby and didn't want to get into the powerhouse job which was about to start. He was very happy to find me to shoulder the responsibilities so that he could be busy with his interest in electronics. We had discussed in detail the progress of the work and plan. I collected some drawings from his office related to the powerhouse and switchyard. We had a few cups of red tea in between. We decided that the next morning, we would be visiting the powerhouse location where the pit excavation was going on.

The head of HR came at that time and we discussed my office arrangement and accommodation. As I had to open my office newly, I requested for supporting staff. I understood that a proper office for me would not be available immediately and two rooms in the adjoining school complex would be provided and a JE to join me shortly. Accommodation would take time. I was happy to be in the guest house as no cooking or cleaning problems would be there. I then visited some other officials of the Dam, spillway, turbine, Power House civil department, and the finance department and as most of them were my contemporaries, they knew me from earlier on. It was 2:30 pm and I reached the guest house for lunch. That day, they made chicken curry but it was full of dry chillies. It was very tasty but I was virtually crying while eating it as it was so hot. I told the cook not to use chilli in my meal and instead give me green chillies separately. They were surprised that people can have a meal without chilli also. I slept until five pm and then decided to go for a walk. The CISF official told me not to cross the gate as the situation in the area was very tense and seven CISF Jawans on duty were martyred one week back inside the project gate. After coming back, I came to know about the whole incident. It was so terrifying.

I took out the drawings to have a preliminary idea of the powerhouse before the visit tomorrow. I slept early. I got up early as the sunlight was directly falling on my face as I had not properly put the curtains the previous night. It was a beautiful morning. The sun was just coming up. I could see the RCE in a white T-shirt and white shorts jogging on the road. He was becoming more and more interesting to me. He was around 70 years of age and fully fit.

FIRST VISIT TO THE POWERHOUSE SITE

I had my breakfast by nine am and was just coming out when my SE reached our guest house driving a green-coloured Gypsy and we started towards the powerhouse location. His driver was seated in the back. We crossed Gate no. 1 and crossed the Doyang Bridge. Then, we took a turn and entered the right bank of the river through Gate no. 2. I was told that the PH was nine km from the Permanent colony (the road was partly under construction, partly completed), where the guest house was located. There was a petrol pump run by my company near Gate no. 2 and that area had some temporary constructions or quarters and was named colony 1. The state bank branch and the civil stores were also located near Gate no. 2, which was manned by the CISF 24×7. We did not wait there and moved toward the powerhouse location. The road within the project was partially boulder pitched and partially blacktopped. After two km from the colony 1, the SE showed me colony 2, which was down the hill and the vehicles could not pass through there.

We reached the zero-point tri-junction. From there, the road diverted in three directions. One went straight ahead to the powerhouse, the second to the Dam, spillway, and switchyard, and the third towards colony 3. On the way to the powerhouse, there was a big field and some construction was going on there. The SE told me that, that would be the powerhouse electrical mechanical stores and would be under me. One km from there, we found the road widening work that was going on and an excavator was working. We were forced to wait for some time. I still vividly remember the scene when I saw a big cobra with its hood raised comfortably resting on the blade of the excavator above the soil it was digging out. Suddenly, some locals came out and killed the beautiful cobra with their *Gulti* (Catapult). My SE told me that Cobra was abundant in Doyang and another surprising thing he told me was that the Naga people cannot withstand snakes and when visible, they would kill them. Later I came to know that it was because of their superstition but it was true. I had some more such incidents later.

Within 500 m from there, we reached the powerhouse location where heavy excavation was going on in full swing. The civil contractor had fully mobilised the area as was apparently seen. BB and the EE PH civil construction were there. There was a temporary CGI sheet-roofed shed being used as a site office. During the discussion, I came to know from the civil contractor that within 10-15 days, they would be in a position to allow the electrical team to start their work.

I had gone down to the pit to see the exact progress myself and was satisfied to find that what they had said in the meeting was achievable. We came back and the SE told me about the CISF incident and showed me the bullet-ridden Gypsy no. NL05 2296 still lying near Gate no. 1 then.

A lot of thought was going on in my head at the same time but I had decided that what may come will come and I had to complete the powerhouse as per the schedule. I decided to establish my office at the earliest, maybe by the next day, if possible, so that I could start my site work as soon as the site was handed over by the civil contractor. I also came to know that the electromechanical erection contractor's project manager had also reached the site. I called him for a discussion the next day. The lunch was quite heavy and I decided to go for a long sleep.

TAKEOVER OF THE OFFICE

The next day, I woke up early and decided to go for a walk. It was quite cold outside and windy as well, forcing me to cancel my programme. I had a good cup of tea instead and started planning my day's activity.

I reached the allotted rooms of my office in the school building with Nath, my driver, and I found the HR in charge was already there with a few workmen to get the rooms cleaned and make my seating arrangements. There was a file cabinet and the room was quite big. The JE had also reported and we three made my office workable. The only thing left was making arrangements for tea in the office, which I needed very frequently. The HR in charge left and I thanked him for all the help. My JE Samuel was in the project for the last few years and I was happy to get a local boy who could help me to carry out my work. Sri. Sitharamaya, project manager of the contractor, reported at around one pm. We started our work plan and discussed mobilisation. He assured me that at least 10 people will report within the next few days and requested space for making their barracks and stores. I told him that I would talk with the CE and shall give him the confirmation tomorrow. It was already 2:30 pm and Samuel and I left for the guest house for lunch.

Samuel and I discussed the project situation while taking lunch and decided to visit the project locations to have a fair idea and to find out space for the contractor's accommodation and stores. Samuel and I stopped first at the store's location, which was nearly complete and some finishing works were only left. Then, we moved to the powerhouse site via colony 3. Almost all Junior Engineers and the Assistant Engineers were accommodated in colony 3. This was the old temporary colony and people gradually shifted to the permanent colony as soon as the permanent buildings were getting ready there, so there were some vacant quarters. I earmarked two quarters, one for me and another for the Erection Contractor's PM and officers. This place would be nearer to the powerhouse site and within a walkable distance of about 1.5 km. We also decided to see the switchyard location and found that the levelling work was going on and would take a few months to be ready. We reached the zero-point (the locations in the projects were named as KM points like zero KM). I dropped Samuel off as he stayed in colony 3 and I had a paan at the zero-point paan shop and came back to the guest house very tired but with a lot of enthusiasm.

I met the CE, BB, the next day and told him that I had identified two quarters in colony 3. He was hesitant to put me in colony 3 as those were in bad shape but I insisted that it would be easier for me to handle my work from there and he ultimately agreed. Both the quarters were allotted accordingly by the HR wing the next day.

I met the Roads & Building EE to do the required renovation of the quarters so that I could occupy them as soon as possible. Within a week, they handed the quarter to me. Luckily, in the meantime, I got a boy Deepak who was about 30 years of age as my housekeeper and cook. Also, my home furniture now reached my house from Golaghat.

Within the next few days, I shifted to my new place. There was a big hall and two rooms with an attached toilet and a room for kitchen cum stores. I occupied one room and the other was given to Deepak and he was very happy. There was no possibility of bringing my family to the project due to the transportation difficulties and I was always busy with my work day and night. Further, the law-and-order situation was extremely bad. A lot of incidents were happening every passing day.

I cannot stress this enough—"the single thing that guarantees a happy, fulfilled and calmer life is the quality of your human relationships, especially the people you love and who love you back". I always missed my family. My wife and my little doll, my daughter, who was only three years old. I decided to keep them with my parents in Golaghat as the situation and the condition of my accommodations were not in good shape for my daughter, at least.

With all set, my office, house, cook, and my driver Nath also staying nearby, my new Doyang establishment was made complete. Now, I was ready for my mission.

THE PROJECT

Doyang HEP is geographically located at $94^0 15' 58''$E longitude and $26^0 13' 47''$N latitude in Wokha district of Nagaland about 26 km north of Wokha town, the district HQ and about 111 km north of Kohima, the State capital. It is located about 70 km from Golaghat town of Assam.

The project site has been selected in the Naga Mountain range. The dam was being constructed across the Doyang river to create the reservoir and between the Lakakishe Hill and its hillocks on the left bank and Chupi Eryo hill and its hillocks on the right bank, respectively. The reservoir covered a total catchment of 2606 sq. km. The site for the powerhouse was selected on the right bank of Doyang at an elevation of 264 m.

The construction of Doyang HEP had been started in February 1983. But due to some unavoidable reasons, the work was stopped and the actual construction works could be started only from mid-1994.

By the time I joined, all the major work fronts like Dam, Spillway, and the powerhouse civil works had started and the Pit excavation was going on. The turbine division had started earth mat laying activities and the draft tube liner of Unit-1 was lowered. However, the excavation for the other two units was still in progress. The civil wing confirmed that they would hand over the Unit-2 area within the next 10-15 days. Very shortly after my joining, the engineer in charge of the Turbine division was transferred and I was told to look after powerhouse Electrical & Mechanical works in totality. It was an enormous task considering the timeline, communication difficulties, and the very small team that was given under my supervision. On attaching the turbine division with me, I was only getting two additional JEs and an Engineer under me and I found them to be very competent and hardworking people.

With all this background, I started planning my activities. First, I pinned two drawings on the display board of my room—the project layout and the powerhouse cross-section—so that I could always refer to them as and when required.

With Samuel and later Piku, Amrit, and Chemchumba Ao, two office staff audio and Beni, I started my office and planned our work. The first priority was in making myself fully informed about the present status and in planning a clear road map for me and my team. For the next two to three days, I sat with my team only discussing the long-term and short-term monthly programme, which was later further refined with discussion with the Erection Contractor.

I found that the turbine generators were ordered and most of the material had reached the Furkating railway station and was kept stored in nearby stores as the transporters were not agreed upon to bring the heavy and over-dimensioned consignments through that road. This was just before my joining.

The powerhouse was designed with an EOT (Electrically operated Travelling) crane for loading or unloading and assembly of heavy items for the powerhouse, which could be moved from one end of the powerhouse to the other end on rails placed at the crane beam at the top. The EOT Crane shipments came in dismantled conditions and the crane girders are placed horizontally at the top. The long girders covered the full width of the powerhouse service bay (the place used for loading or unloading and the assembly of heavy items) and the turbine division had started transporting both the girders of the powerhouse EOT crane but, unfortunately, at the foothills of

Merapani at almost nearby locations, both the girders had gone down the hill and were lying around 200-250 ft. down the hill.

We had found that to do the project, the most critical activity was the safe transportation of the heavy over-dimensioned consignment from Furkating store to the project site. That was very risky but we had no alternative. Risk had to be taken as Lee Iacocca once said, "even a correct decision is wrong when it was taken too late."

With this in mind, we had decided to start with recovering the girders lying at the foothills before the start of the monsoon rain. I met the CE and requested his help in cutting and repairing the very sharp curves at the foothills and to fill the pits with some sand and gravel so that the transportation could be attempted. The CE called SE Roads & Buildings (R&B) and we discussed what could be done. As decided, SE, R&B, and myself with my team went to the foothills for a joint inspection the next day early in the morning. We found that a very small portion of the bend could only be cut but the pits could be filled with sand gravel. Accordingly, work was started and some improvements could be made to the curves but the curves and the gradient were still very sharp. Having no other alternative, we decided to recover the crane girders first to test ourselves.

With this in mind, my team again started to the location with some of our truck drivers, Mobile crane operators, and some labourers along with us to plan how the work could be done. We took the whole day at that site and drew a detailed plan, including who would do what. The next day, I told the CE that I planned to do the work departmentally and he encouraged me. I was sure that unless this was done, the powerhouse work couldn't progress. Those girders were a test for us and if we could do it, it would give confidence to my team to carry the balance heavy equipment. Another big hurdle was that telephone connectivity was not available within the project and communication with HQ took place through

Wireless transmission (WT) or one had to come to Golaghat or Kohima to make a call. All my team, including the R&B team, prepared all materials as per the checklist, including the material for preparing food at the road site. It seemed that all my team members were good cooks, too.

START OF A MISSION

We started at three am the next day from the project site as soon as we were ready with our preparation and reached the location at around six am. After some time, our 40 T Mobile Crane with driver Das and Gogoi also reached the site. The crane was brought from the Kopili project and was kept at CRPF camp five km downhill in Assam-Nagaland boundary. Two dumpers were deployed to carry sand and boulders to fill the road wherever required.

By the time people had reached the girder at the downhill location—by going down the hill slope with the help of rope—and tied the girder with a steel wire sling, it was around 11:30 am. The girder's weight was only 6 T but its length was a cause for worry while carrying it in an ordinary truck. I was worried that while dragging the girder, the crane should not overturn. We bound the crane with a heavy sling in two big trees in the back and Das-our crane operator- started his machine. The traffic on the road was negligible and was mainly only our project vehicles and we had stopped plying our project vehicles for the day. Everyone was praying. Around 50 ft, the girder was moving up easily as the slope was good but after that, it started giving trouble as some trees and the slope was obstructing. By the time it reached the road, it was six pm. Everybody was shouting in happiness only to realise then that none had taken any food until then. Quickly, Khichdi was made on the roadside and we had our breakfast and lunch cum dinner at around nine pm.

Now, the next part was to put the girder in the truck and to carry it to the project. Sri. Paul, the most expert driver of the project, took the lead in loading the material and properly fastened it in his truck with everyone following his order. I found him quite confident that he could carry the same in his normal truck; even though I had some doubt initially, seeing his confident face, I agreed. I knew the officials, after such a hectic day, needed some break and I told them to wait for an hour before starting to project. I knew most of them had some liquor and were feeling relaxed.

We started back to the project with one escort vehicle leading two dumpers with sand and gravel and the driver Paul was next with the girder in his truck, followed by 40 T mobile crane and an excavator. I with my officers were last in the convoy in two jeeps.

After reaching Bagti around two am, Driver Das and Excavator driver decided to spend the balance of the night at Bagti as they were very tired. We left them there and proceeded to the project.

By the time I reached the guest house, it was five am. The sun was already up. I was exhausted but also relaxed thinking about the first successful transportation mission. I straightway went to the bed. Looking back today, it seemed to be a small job but considering the resources available at that time and the road conditions and gradients, it was really a big milestone achieved and gave the much-required confidence to my entire team.

Dhiren called me up at 10:30 am, telling me that my CE and SE were waiting for me in the guest house lobby. I jumped out of the bed and reached the lobby. All were so happy. I was really encouraged.

After two days, we planned for our next mission to recover the next girder lying in the foothills. The same process was followed and the girder was successfully loaded into the truck and driver Paul followed the two dumpers with the sand gravel and the crane followed. The excavator was left there to attend to some road work the next day. Our two jeeps, with all my officials, were at the last.

We were proceeding at a very slow speed to match the speed of the mobile Crane. After some time, our driver Nath decided to go a bit faster and overtook the mobile crane to wait later, as otherwise, it would have been very tiring and boring.

We moved only about five to six km from Bhandari gate and had halted there to wait for the crane. We waited there for an hour but there was no sign of the crane. We were very worried and when a private truck came from that direction, we stopped him and asked him if he had seen the crane. The driver told us that he had not seen any crane on the road. We got scared as the Crane was quite big and no one could miss seeing it on the way. Without waiting for my instruction, Nath took our vehicle back. All were speechless and we only worried that the crane might have gone downhill. All of us were looking down both sides of the road while returning. We were about to reach Bhandari point when the driver's assistant "Gogoi" came running to us. We were so frightened and made ourselves ready to hear any bad news.

He told us that there was a road diversion at that location. One going up leading to some government quarters that lead to a dead-end and the other road going to our project. Das had mistakenly taken the other diversion, going up the hill towards the quarters and after getting to the dead end, he understood his mistake and turned the crane in that narrow space but had accidentally damaged the roof of a quarter made of CGI sheets while doing it. Unfortunately, that was the quarter of a senior police officer and he was in a state of shock for having that sudden attack on his house. The area was most insurgency prone and something or the other happened there regularly. After getting the fact of the matter, he seized the Crane. We were all relaxed that our people and the Crane, all were safe and we went to the location only about 400-500 m uphill and I told my Engineer Piku to talk to the Police officer in their native language. But the officer was not listening to anything and went on giving all kinds of dirty scolding to us and did not allow us to take the Crane even after our promise that by morning, our project team would come and repair all the damages to his quarter. He was fully drunk. I was looking at all of this happening in front of me and decided to intervene. I introduced myself and talked to him but he was only interested in cash compensation. I asked Piku to keep him busy in the discussion with him. In the meantime, I told Das, the crane operator, to reverse the crane and take it slowly to the road. The drunken officer went inside after some time. By that time, the crane was on the road 500 m down and hurriedly, we left the place. We did not stop anywhere till Bagti and went at the maximum possible speed. The crane operators Das and Gogoi were too exhausted and I told them to sleep there. We proceeded and reached the project gate at 6:45 am. Driver Paul with the girder reached much earlier. From the gate, I contacted the CE and told him what had happened. He immediately arranged a team with material and sent it to the house at Bhandari to get the damage repaired but the officer did not allow any repair and demanded only cash compensation. So, our people returned without any repair work done. I asked all my team members to take complete rest and we did not discuss anything, including unloading. The whole day, I took rest by only eating and sleeping, feeling as if it were the next day after a marriage was over. It was really exhausting and we were all fully drained and, especially, the last episode had been dramatic. The RCE solved the matter of the damage to the house through his contact in Kohima so that our people did not face any problem moving through the Bhandari gate.

We had decided that before starting the Unit work, we would finish the erection of the EOT crane at least up to the service bay to make loading or unloading of the heavy material and their assembly easier. I had requested my civil counterpart, my SE and CE to pursue with the civil contractor to make the crane beam ready, and if required, the Unit work going on in the civil construction site might be deferred. After a lot of follow-ups, ultimately, after a month, the EOT crane beam concreting was done and we got the EOT Crane beam ready for the crane erection 28 days thereafter. As soon as the beam concreting was completed, we had given notice to the contractor to mobilise and we started shifting the material to the service bay area for starting the Erection work.

The girders were placed safely over the beam at the top. But to erect the motors, we had a big problem as the service bay roof was not ready and it would take substantial time, which we could not afford. So, we decided to go ahead without the roof. The next day, we lifted the motors to the top and made them ready for the erection. It was 8:30 pm and I told my team to call it a day so that the balance work could be done the next morning. The weather was perfectly alright and I decided to go home. Before I left, I told my Engineer Piku to cover the motors properly, even though the weather was alright. He agreed and I left for my quarter. By the time I reached home, lightning started. I rang Piku over the intercom but there was no reply. I immediately drove to the powerhouse again and found that Piku was carrying a big tarpaulin over his head and going up to the crane top through a temporary iron ladder with one labour assisting him. As soon as he covered the motors, heavy rain started. After half an hour, he came down and I felt so bad when he told me, "Sir, your motors are safe but your Engineer is fully drenched!" I was overwhelmed seeing his involvement in his duty that I simply hugged him. I was then hundred percent confident that with this small team, I would be able to complete my mission.

The old medical building at zero km point was lying vacant for a long time. From there, the powerhouse was a kilometre away and the store was in the front. I requested the CE to allot this building to me for my office. He agreed and I shifted to this building; it was a temporary construction but was still in a good condition. Later, the civil sub-division officer of the powerhouse also shifted to this building. I continued my office in this building till I was transferred in 2001. It was a good place at the hilltop but without any security arrangements.

MATERIAL TRANSPORTATIONS

As soon as I took over the charge of the powerhouse, I understood that material transportation was the toughest part of the project and if the same can be done successfully, half the work of the project can be treated as complete. All projects have different types of criticalities and here it was the transportation of the heavy materials under the most difficult law and order situation prevailing at that time and the road condition, which was identified as the most severe by me and my team.

With this in mind, we started making an elaborate plan, discussion after discussion. First, we listed the material requirements as per the sequence of the erection activity. The list was with the dimension and weight of the consignment. The need for a special trailer or truck was also worked out. Lifting and the loading-unloading arrangement were a part of our plan.

We got only a few months to transport materials due to the weather conditions, so planning was very important. Luckily, we had successfully recovered and brought the EOT crane girders from the foothills, which had given us a lot of confidence and after the crane was commissioned, the unloading issues at the site were also resolved.

Now, we were planning to take on the bigger consignments. Bringing the Generator stator segments lying at the Furkating store was the biggest challenge, so the first major item to be transported to the site was selected as the generator stator segments. We had requisitioned the 40 T mobile crane from our Kopili Project, which reached Furkating after 10-15 days and Driver Das and Gogoi, who was put as his assistant, had brought the crane from Kopili Project to Furkating.

The Transporter was selected and the contractor shortly mobilised their heavy-duty low-bed trailer at the Furkating store. With all in place as planned, we decided to carry out our mission of transporting heavy and over-dimensioned consignments one by one before the start of the monsoon rain. The selected stator segments were 30 T in weight but they were an over-dimensioned consignment. There were altogether nine segments for the three units.

As planned, the first segment was loaded in the trailer at Furkating, which consumed almost a day and we decided to move it to the foothills so that by the next day early morning, it would be ready to be moved to the project site. The trailer reached Merapani CRPF camp at around nine pm and we decided to go back to our Furkating transit camp so that we could start early in the morning, the next day.

We reached early morning at Merapani and had our breakfast there at Sarmah's stall. The convoy consisted of one Gypsy with a local leader Sharao Jami, who was leading the convoy to stop the vehicle coming from the opposite side, followed by two trucks with sand and gravel to fill the potholes on the way. Next followed the 42-wheeler low-bed trailer, carrying the first segment of the stator to the project site. We started from the CRPF camp around five km from the foothills. The 40 T mobile crane was to follow the trailer to help negotiate the curves by dragging the back of the trailer where necessary and then our team followed in two wide-bodied jeeps. All reached the foothills safely and waited there for some time before starting the uphill curves. The trailer started moving up and we were yet to be in our jeep to see how things proceeded. For about half a kilometre, the trailer was moving smoothly but then suddenly, everything was in chaos and the trailer was coming down on its own. All were in a state of panic. I shouted to all my team members to throw stones at the tyres of the trailer from a dump of stone on the roadside. Suddenly, the trailer stopped with less than a metre before hitting the hill at the back to everyone's relief. Most of the tyres of the trailer had gotten burst but we were happy that the consignment was saved so miraculously. The next big issue was that the trailer stopped in such a way that the road got blocked. We put boulders in all the tyres so that they could not move downslide again. With the help of the mobile crane, we dragged the front of the trailer towards the hill so that the vehicles could just pass.

With all this, we were all speechless for some time and did not know how one of the costliest consignments was saved. Only God had helped us. If anything bad happened, I could have been held responsible as all planning and site supervision was happening under my leadership. We recovered from the shock after some time. We all went back to Merapani. The driver of the trailer was terrified by the incident. At Merapani, we took paratha as usual and tea. Then, we went to Golaghat leaving a few people for the security of the trailer after arranging food for those people and the drivers who wanted to be with the trailer.

It was now understood that the 50 T prime mover of the trailer was not sufficient to pull the consignment in such a curve with a sharp gradient and needed additional pulling capacity. We had a 50 T Mac prime mover at our Kopili project and we requested our HQ Shillong to send the same to Merapani immediately. In the morning, we sent some of our people to the project as our bosses could have been worried about us. No telephone was available at the project, so we needed to report directly to ask for any help.

After two days, the prime mover reached Merapani and on the same day, the transporter arranged the replacement tyres. But the changing of tyres took a full day and, on its completion, we started again. This time, our 50 T prime mover pulled the trailer's prime mover from the front, followed by the 40 T mobile crane to help negotiate the curves.

This time, the trailer was moving quite decently and only in a few locations did the back of the trailer had to be dragged by the mobile crane so that it could negotiate the curve better. Within two hours, we crossed the hill section and reached the Bhandari check gate. There were people all along to see the convoy, most probably that was a rare occasion even for me. One Gypsy to stop vehicles from the opposite side, two dumpers for putting sand and boulders at the potholes, 50 T prime mover pulling the prime mover of the 42-wheeler low bed trailer, then the 40 T crane, and two of our jeeps. We missed our cameras badly. We felt very relaxed after reaching Bhandari and we told the drivers of the trailers to slowly move and halt at Bagti, which was on a plain road so that the next day, we could take care of the balance distance that had downward and narrow curves near Sanis. The others went back to the project. The Gypsy was sent earlier to the project for bringing some food for the drivers who were to halt at Bagti and some security manpower for the vehicles, men, and materials.

The next day, we started from the project early. We kept some people in our guest house so that they could carry some food to the people stranded at Bagti overnight. After having breakfast at Bagti, we started our Project transportation. The road was plain and there was no problem up to Sanis from where the downward slope started and the road became narrow. Now and then, the trailer had to be dragged by the mobile crane at the back of the trailer for negotiating the curves. However, with all these new experiences for all of us, the first stator segment reached the powerhouse location and was safely unloaded at the service bay with the help of the newly erected EOT crane.

All started shouting *Bihu songs* and were dancing in jubilation forgetting everything. All senior officials reached the powerhouse site and congratulated us. By the time we reached home, it was quite late and Dipak was waiting at my colony 3 quarter with dinner and

Mr. Deb, who was my colleague and Executive Engineer of the Workshop Division, was waiting with a few bottles of drinks, which were so badly needed by all of us. We were taking special care of the drivers, who were the heroes and they were provided accommodation at the guest house.

The trailers needed some repairs and the next day, the arrangement was made to get the heavy trailers repaired at our workshop. Some parts were required to be brought from Guwahati as those spares were normally not available in our stores. Within a week, we were all ready for the second mission. Before the rain started, we completed safely moving six segments from Furkating to Project and we had to stop as the rain had already started and the road further deteriorated.

We were to carry the bottom brackets to the site so that there was no disruption of erection activities for at least one unit. The transporter was told to send a shorter trailer as there was a landslide near Sanis and even though the Bottom Bracket consignment was a heavy consignment, it was not over-dimensioned. However, the transporter sent the consignment in a long trailer. It was carried by the same way, of course, without our 40 T mobile crane—which was sent back to Kopili as there was some urgent need for it there—up to Sanis but the long trailer could not negotiate the curves at Sanis and we were compelled to stop there. Further, we did not have the mobile crane with us. The trailer got stranded for nearly a week when the transporter sent one shorter trailer from Guwahati to Sanis. The problem arose as there was no high-capacity crane with us at that time or nearby to hire for shifting from the longer to the shorter trailer. Ultimately, some innovative ways were applied and both the trailers were put side-by-side matching and almost touching each other. With the hydraulic jack from the power station, we lifted the bottom bracket by six inches and put the transformer yard rail at the bottom of the bracket. The rail shared both the trailers so that the consignment could be dragged by winch from one to the other dragging. As planned, we acted accordingly. Now if I think back, I find it quite funny as nowadays for handling heavy machinery, all facilities are available even in Merapani also and these can be hired easily with much better road conditions. But 30 years back, people did not even have any idea about the existence of such transportation machinery. That time, people were running to see our jeeps. Thirty years is quite a long time in technology and communication. What we have to do or are compelled to do, the present generation of Engineers cannot even think of or are required to think of. However, we did not have any alternative but to do all these to complete our mission of the commissioning of the Doyang project successfully and on time.

After a whole day's exercise, the consignment was shifted from the longer trailer to the shorter one, which could now negotiate the curves. From there, it was downhill and there was no problem with pulling. The trailer reached the powerhouse around two am and by the time we reached home, the sun God had already come out.

The Trailer was in the powerhouse for two days before unloading as most of my people got sick after that operation, then after unloading, the trailer was sent back duly escorted by our officials.

The rain had already started and the road became fully muddy and unpliable. Our Mission transportation, therefore, had to stop there for the time being till the monsoon was over in October. But we had achieved major success and experience and there would be no hindrance to the erection of the first two units. I had taken a sigh of relief.

EVENING IN COLONY 3

Colony 3 was a temporary construction that was made 10-12 years back and most of the quarters were in a bad shape. I had occupied quarter no. 1A and another Senior Engineer Deb was in my front quarter no. 2A. There were about 40 quarters in the colony. Almost all were occupied by the project's middle-level Engineers, Junior Engineers Assistant Engineers, and contractors' Project Managers.

The senior officials, except for Deb and I, had already shifted to the permanent colony. I preferred colony 3 as it was near to my site and it reduced my unnecessary travels. All the Junior Engineers were young bachelors and were full of enthusiasm. I was also a forced bachelor as due to the prevailing situation there, my family could not be brought. My Engineer Piku was also staying nearby my quarter. There were also quarters for drivers and other skilled workmen nearby.

Normally, in the project, the civil works started early in the day and as they left very early to the site, they also came back early. Our work normally started a bit late but we preferred to work till late as, after the departure of the civil teams, working was more convenient and safer as both were working in the same space. Deb maintained office time from nine am to five pm (normal office timing and was in charge of workshop division) and he normally was the first one to return from office to home or reach our sites and was with us till our return. We normally reached back around nine pm, unless there was any continuous process going on, in which case we normally worked late till the process was completed.

One day when I reached home, I found that my residence was fully occupied by all the engineers of our colony. All were sitting on the floor and all the young engineers were enjoying singing Bihu or Hindi film songs and dancing. I was surprised but was very happy with the environment. Later, my cook Deepak told me that Deb had arranged the same and called everybody. It continued till late at night. I also joined. After that night, it became almost routine and the Musical Nights were continued by our dedicated Junior Engineers or Assistant Engineers who considered Deb and me as their elder brothers. I was very happy with them as all were very hard workers and they were very disciplined and sincere officers and never said no to what we told them to do without giving it a try. Everyone tried to help each other and the unity amongst the team was exemplary.

This was rare and unique and a very special characteristic of the Doyang project team. Because of the external threats of the insurgency and local goons, the people were not moving alone and always moved in teams. Sometimes, the contractor's project manager Sitharamaya and his officers also joined in our get-togethers. I noticed that some of our engineers used to suddenly go out to Deb's quarter in my front and came back after some time. It seemed that everybody needed some relaxation after a hard day's work with all kinds of problems and I understood that they were taking a few pegs, which were stored in Deb's place and came back to join the mehfil again. They were scared to take it in front of me and hence made this special arrangement. Taking a few pegs made them relaxed and made them fit for the next day's schedule. I did not interfere. But these young boys were so well-behaved and dedicated and they treated me as their elder brother, which amazed me. During duty hours, they maintained full discipline and never took advantage of the fact that we sang and enjoyed ourselves together in the evening at my house.

Deb told me later the actual reason for arranging this gathering. If you are alone in the quarter, some unauthorised person in the name of an insurgent group would come to your house demanding work, money, etc. and might create panic situations. These happened even in presence of security officials who proved themselves as very ineffective after the December incident at gate no. 1. Paramilitary forces were having their camp inside the campus. To avoid trouble from these people, the best strategy was to be together as much as possible and the result was these musical evenings.

DOYANG SWITCHYARD

The switchyard area was handed over to us after levelling as scheduled. The Erection Contractor started mobilizing. Almost all materials were received at the site, including the 5MVA,132/33 kV transformer, and the transportation of the same took place with several difficulties at the foothills. The construction drawings were released by our design wing. We found that there were serious mistakes in the drawing when we started marking for the excavation of foundations. The Isolators could foul the tower during the opening operations. I informed our Design and HQ regarding the issue and requested a visit of the Designers. After a 10-15 days' delay, our Design Engineer and Consultant reached the site. I explained the problem but they were not ready to accept their mistakes. The next day, I took them to the site but there also, their attitude was like Greats who couldn't make mistakes and they behaved with the "I know everything and we have made no mistakes" type of attitude. We had some heated arguments at the site and I felt very bad. I told them to at least listen to the problem we were facing but they were blaming everything on us. I was very angry and simply asked them to leave the site as they were not even ready to discuss the matter and to forget about the solutions. I always believed that Project Engineering is a team business and there would only be advantages if the team discusses before starting any work, which will give them a clear direction for taking quick decisions.

I briefed our CE, BB, and with his permission, I left for Golaghat the next morning to make a phone call to our CE Generation at the corporate office as he was a master in such design matters. I was lucky to work under him before my transfer to Doyang and he knew me very well. I had a habit of not accepting things till I am convinced that the same will work. Till then, I normally went on asking questions to everyone concerned, including myself. CE, GP knows that very well and encouraged me with such inquisitiveness. I told him everything and he understood instantly. He was sure that there must be a major problem in the drawings; otherwise, I normally never escalated issues to his level. He advised me not to take any action till he came to the site within the next two days. Accordingly, we kept the site closed for two days till his arrival. He reached Doyang at around nine pm two days later as scheduled. After breakfast on the next day, we reached the site. We started for the switchyard site with Samuel, my Junior Engineer. In the location, CE(GP) read the drawings and asked me to explain the problem and I detailed it to him. He asked for a measuring tape and one end of the tape was taken by him to my utter astonishment and the other side by me. Samuel was noting down the readings. In the present-day circumstances, if I say that the CE Generation, who was one of the topmost in the hierarchy, was taking measurements with an Executive Engineer at the site, no one will believe so. Nowadays, it is very rare to find such senior officials without any ego and I have seen this in almost so many organisations—the team of flatterers gains more importance in the power structure and people at the decision-making level are unable to know the exact difficulties and situations faced by the site engineers or the progress made, even if they know its solutions. Their visit to the site, therefore, becomes a mere formality and is rarely of use in finding solutions to the problems. But people like our CE, GP, of that time always went to the details and helped the site officials to take the correct and quick decisions without much ado. During that period, we were having such senior officials from whom we learned so many things; they never showed their ego and were always ready to help us at the time when we faced any problem. We were very fortunate, really.

I had to face another difficulty as I did not have a senior experienced electrical mechanical man in the project with whom I could discuss matters. When one is not interested or involved, discussing a problem with them is just a waste of time, if not more. I also gradually reduced meetings with such people and reported to our project CE, BB from whom I got all kinds of support. Some of my project seniors found me difficult to handle and avoided me and normally visited the powerhouse when they knew I was not there and gave a lot of instruction to my young Engineers. They got confused as most of the instructions were not as per the team's decisions. I told them to keep an instruction register there. Anyone who wanted to give instruction should give it in writing. The number of instructions stopped automatically. The RCE and the other officers knew me very well and that I would not tolerate any lapses during the work process and my juniors respected me because I always gave them the chance to learn and to take all responsibility. They knew that for solving problems, discussion amongst the team was very much essential, which I always encouraged them to do. I had given my team all freedom to work but warned them that they should not tell me lies or hide such facts and if they made a mistake, I would take all responsibility for their decisions as long as they kept me informed about the same on time.

CE, GP then again checked the drawings and was convinced that what I told him was correct. He asked me what my plan was. In the meantime, I had made a drawing during the last two days, which I produced for him. He read it very carefully and agreed with what I was suggesting. There itself he put the paper on my Gypsy bonnet and wrote on the drawing "approved and released for construction." He had such a sharp brain and was a very decisive person. I bow down to officers like him. Before lunch, we came back to the guest house where our project CE, the RCE, and other senior officials were waiting for him. We had our lunch together and our CE Generation projects left for Golaghat in the evening. After his departure, all of us talked about him and all had only praise and regard for him, such a humble and down-to-earth man he was.

We restarted the switchyard (SY) work soon. Doyang SY was a relatively big switchyard, having 9 bays of 132 kV and a 132/33 kV system for supply to work sites, which were then supplied power through Diesel generating sets. It also had a 33/11 kV system for Unit auxiliary requirements.

SHIFTING TO A PERMANENT COLONY

In the meantime, some quarters were made ready for Senior officers and on BB's insistence, I had to shift to the permanent colony after nearly one and half years at colony 3. I felt very bad as we really had a team who were all full of youthful energy and were together as a family but I could not say no to BB. Deb decided to stay where he was as he was about to retire shortly.

My quarter was at the hilltop and in the same block as that of the RCE's. For my every movement, I had to cross the RCE's residence. My new quarter was a big one with two big rooms, a kitchen, dining hall, etc. Much bigger than people like me without family required. In Doyang, most of the officers did not keep their families with them as there was no proper educational facility and the situation was not at all congenial. Only during long holidays, the families normally visited them for a few days. BB, SE dam and spillway, SE R&B, and my SE kept their family at the project as their children were staying in hostels outside. Others were mostly forced bachelors.

We five—Pranab, Tilak, Jeet, Sapan, and I—stayed at the hilltop accommodations, a VIP guest house converted into quarters. Sapan and Jeet kept their families with them. Both of them had a boy child each, Vivek and Raj, and they were around five years of age. A badminton court was in the front of our quarter.

Shortly, Deepak made all the arrangements for the kitchen and I shifted to my new house. That time, my old wide-bodied Jeep was replaced by a better-conditioned Willys Jeep without doors. There was no garage for parking and we parked our vehicles in the badminton court area only. One day, in the morning, I was about to go to the powerhouse site and I was talking in a loud voice to Sapan who was standing outside his house. Without noticing anything, I sat in the driver's seat, turned on the engine and I tried to move the gear lever. I then felt something very cold in my hand. I saw a green viper coiled in the gear lever. I jumped out of the vehicle, leaving the gear maybe in neutral. I placed a brick on the wheels so that the vehicle would not move on its own. I was so terrified by this incident and I was scared to sit in the driver's seat for some time. Sapan and all had come but the snake took his own time to leave the vehicle. Must be he was also under a shock. There were so many snakes in the area, either green vipers or different species of cobra. I had a lot of encounters with them.

One day, one of my Engineers was accompanying me and I was driving. Suddenly, a big cobra crossed the road and I had to slow down. My Engineer, who was a local boy and was a very cold and simple guy, suddenly got out of the car, followed the cobra, and killed it. I remembered what my SE told me once then.

ATTACK ON THE RCE'S LIFE

It was about seven in the morning. Deepak called me from my sleep and told me, "Sir, something had happened in the RCE's house and all people are gathering there." I jumped out of my bed and came out. I saw a lot of local people with their *Daos* and spears returning downhill through a small pathway normally not used by anyone, shouting something in unison in their local dialect. Tilak and I ran to the RCE's bungalow and found that the RCE was lying in a pool of blood and it was coming out of his head profusely. He was taken to a chair and Dr. Mrs. Mao and sister Miano started cleaning and stitching his wound to save him so that he can at least be shifted to Golaghat. We were all dumbfounded to do anything. We saw the RCE still in his senses, telling us not to worry and to go to our site and not to stop working. The CE construction management from HQ arrived at Doyang the previous night and was in the guest house. Hearing the news, he also reached there. Within a few minutes, whole project officials were in the RCE's Bungalow. Our priority was to shift him to Golaghat at the earliest as our Doyang hospital was not equipped for such major casualties. After an hour, he was sent to Golaghat and Dr. Mrs. Mao accompanied him along with other officials who moved in advance and along with him. He reached Golaghat safely and after the preliminary treatment, he was referred to Guwahati as his condition was serious. CE (CM) was a very worried person and he was frightened, even though he was trying to give us confidence but the whole incident made everybody shaky. All work fronts automatically came to a grinding halt. This happened when all kinds of security forces were present in the Project and the corporation was spending huge money on them. The CE (CM) told us that he will go to Golaghat for some phone call and shall come back but he did not come back and all were very offended for the same as we all expected that he being the senior-most would lead us during this critical hour. His absence created a lot of resentment. Through WT, we came to know that the RCE reached Guwahati safely and was admitted to the hospital and that he was stable. We were a bit relaxed with the news. He was the fatherly figure in the project and commanded everybody's respect.

All the officers and staff decided to stop working unless proper safety was provided for the employees. People were in various groups discussing what had happened. Some senior officials, including CE Ranganadi Project, were deputed to the site from HQ to convince the officials but he failed. After this, he threatened action and people became more agitated and adamant that he had to leave the site seeing the mood of the employees. None joined duty but all remained at the project. After around 10 days, the project engineers got an appointment with the highest authority of the state and the meeting was held in Kohima, the state capital. A lot of assurance was given but the culprits were not apprehended even though their names were known. Things were not improving.

In the meantime, the RCE gradually recovered and was discharged from the hospital and he came back to his house in Kohima. He also requested all of us to resume duty but none was prepared to join unless proper security was provided. The existing security was defunct. Very Senior bureaucrats of the central home ministry came and after their visit, some additional reinforcement was made. We decided to go back to duty and the situation gradually came back to normalcy but every day something or the other was happening in the project area. People were scared to move. With this ground situation, all of us decided that by any means, we had to commission the project as soon as possible and get out as transfer demand at that stage was not possibly be agreed upon by the management and if the management wanted to post someone to

Doyang, they found it more convenient to resign. Reinforcement of additional force had no meaning as they did not act when necessary and people had to care for themselves by themselves.

As a result, we all became more and more involved in our job and we were in a hurry to complete the project. All the contractors were also putting all their efforts to expedite. In other words, the situation was very tense but everybody kept the work front going as fast as possible.

LIFE IN THE PERMANENT COLONY

During that time, Bhupen, a Senior Engineer, joined my team and he was given a quarter at D type in a permanent colony near the church. He started taking food together with me at my house and was very happy with what Deepak prepared. Deepak used to take some kind of *Nasha*, we actually do not know, but we always found him sleeping. He stayed alone the full day as we went out in the morning, came for lunch, and again went to the site and there was no fixed timing as to when we came back but he used to be busy with his favourite hobby. At dinner, he always did something peculiar, maybe in his *Nasha*, and he even usually didn't know what he had prepared. Pranab also had a cook Bhaity and after we came back from the site, we used to sit on the floor and both Bhaity and Deepak used to bring their preparations. We three, and sometimes Tilak, also joined us in our grand dinner. Normally, Pranab came earlier and waited for us to come back. Our badminton game also started late at night and there was no fixed time for our activities, be it the game, taking lunch, or going to the site. We never maintained a routine for our safety as people could not predict our movements, including the drivers, as we used to drive on our own.

By the time we finished our dinner, Jeet normally came with a steel bowl and spoon as his musical instrument and we started our music session till late at night with Jeet's special accompaniment. Bhupen was an excellent guitarist. Our Mazlis normally continued till midnight and we forgot all our problems and the day's tiring activities.

Tilak was a very good singer and he sang *Bhupen Hazarika, Rabha, Jyoti sangeet,* and the old Hindi songs very well. Pranab and I were good for nothing in music and were only helping the performers with a line or two in the middle and playing the drum on our wooden tables. Surprisingly, Tilak knew the lyrics of all the songs from the start to finish and had an elephant's memory; Sapan also joined sometimes, but after a few minutes, he had to leave as his wife would shout calling him back. Poor fellow! She thought we were drinking, which we normally did only after having some big thing accomplished and never as a routine. BB and his wife also came sometimes to play rummy in Pranab's house. My SE and also SE Dam and spillway along with his wife would come to enjoy. She never played rummy and she was the very sweet jolly type of woman and was very talkative. Everyone enjoyed her presence on any occasion as she kept everyone in good humour. She was a very good cook, too. If we happened to visit them, we were fed so much till we shouted not to give any more. SE, D&S, always enjoyed but never spoke anything and go on smiling.

FAMILY FRONT

Kakoli, my wife, was carrying and expecting sometime in the last week of August. As my cousin was a Gynaecologist and he had a nursing home of his own, I was a little bit comfortable. However, as August started, I was getting a bit restless. I visited my house in August first week and had her check-up done. The doctor maintained that the expected date would be the last week of that month. But after the ceremony on 15th August at the project—that year, I had to unfurl the national flag due to the absence of my seniors—and once the celebrations were over, I left for Golaghat in the evening. Kakoli was fine and we took a walk to the market the next day in the evening. We had our dinner and went to bed by eleven pm. Suddenly, around two am she called me and told me she needed to go to a nursing home as she had serious pain. I did not think it was real and told her to sleep till the morning and that we would see what was required to be done then.

But by 3:30 am, she was having serious pain and I had to shift her to the nursing home and give a call to my cousin. Within half an hour, he reached and checked her up. He told me to be relaxed and he said he was expecting the delivery to happen midday only and that all was fine. I went straight to my uncle's house and brought my Aunty *Mami* to the nursing home. It was still dark. I was waiting in the nursing home till my mother arrived. There was a canteen in the nursing home and I took puri bhaji and my Mami also wanted to be in the hospital. I went home and brought the breakfast cum lunch for them. The doctor visited two to three times and around 1:30 pm, she was shifted to the labour room. We all were waiting anxiously outside. It was around 2:30 pm when a lady nurse came out of the labour room and congratulated me and asked for new clothes for the baby who was a boy. We have given her the same which was kept ready. But after 15 minutes or so, she again came and asked for clothes as a second baby boy was born. We were all dumbfounded as the doctor never told us it would be a twin. I immediately rushed to the market and got those clothes and gave them to the nurse. We were still waiting outside. After some time, the doctor came out. I was very angry with him as he did not inform us earlier. He was laughing and told me if you were informed what else would you have done except for having 10 more cigarettes. He knew that from earlier on and that was why he came at four am to the hospital and all medical care was personally supervised by him.

All in the family were very happy. God helped me as I was not supposed to come home that day but suddenly, I had. If I was not there, a lot of difficulties could have been faced by my wife. It was a normal delivery and she was released from the nursing home within a few days.

In August 97', my father suddenly became very sick and required to be hospitalised. I had to take leave, giving my charge to Bhupen. But my father's condition was not improving. Doctors had advised me to take him home as there was no more treatment possible except for pushing saline and some injections for giving him some temporary relief.

But he did not come out of his sickness and left us within a very short period. Everyone including my mother, my sisters, brothers-in-law, and my family were with him in the early morning of 17th September 97' when he left us. I lost my best friend and adviser who always stood with me and inspired me.

Within a few weeks of my father's passing, my wife had an accident—she fell in the room itself and broke her knee. Fortunately, I was at home that day also and took her to the hospital. She was not in a position to stand up and hence with a lot of difficulties, she was taken to a nursing home. The surgeon Dr. Baruah was a very nice gentleman and he operated on her and removed the patella which was broken into several pieces. She was required to be in hospital for a few days before her discharge. On the home front, my twins were just about to be a year old and my daughter was only four. My mother had just come out of the shock of my father's death. But she and my mother-in-law somehow managed the home front as I had to be with my wife at the hospital. Whoever came to my house felt bad about the situation and wanted to lend a helping hand. People were coming with some domestic help, which was very difficult to find and as for how long they stayed, there was no guarantee. I kept whoever was coming and as a result, I had five domestic help appointed at that time and my mother had the additional burden of cooking for them also. My wife was discharged with the advice to perform some physiotherapy exercises regularly. But after a month also, she did not fully recover. So, I took her to Guwahati to the best orthopaedic surgeon at that time. He did another operation and released her after a few days and we came back. She was doing the exercises and soon recovered. Some bad days had gone by and I was not in touch with the project for quite some time but Bhupen was managing well and giving me relief from the project-related issues for some time.

SARASWATI PUJA AT PROJECT

With all those tensions of law-and-order issues and the routine incidences of terror activities, Saraswati puja was celebrated with much fanfare in the project traditionally from the beginning. The Finance department organised the same at the Recreational club complex auditorium. There was puja in the daytime with Khichdi at lunch for all and in the evening, a grand musical night was organised. That year, a troop from Kolkata was invited and the auditorium was full.

The compere of the troop gave some boring lectures in between and the performance was also not at all entertaining. The people were getting impatient and the crowd started shouting. Bhupen was impatient too and was very angry with the performers and at last, he could not keep his cool. There was an announcement that the Kolkata team would come back after some break soon after the performance by our local artist who was nobody other than Bhupen himself on the stage, one musician from the Kolkata party on drums and Bhaity to help Bhupen on stage. He started playing his guitar, one beautiful piece after another. Suddenly, the atmosphere changed and everybody was loving his guitar. He went on playing one hit song after another. People were shouting "Once more!" and dancing to the tunes.

By the time he was off the stage and the Kolkata team re-entered, the people started leaving and the hall was empty soon. It was such an enthralling performance by Bhupen—my colleague, brother, and friend—who had recently joined my team.

***

I was frequently going to Golaghat due to the condition at my house during that time. I got a phone call from my CE, GP from Shillong at my house—that time, Golaghat was connected by telephone services and I was fortunate to have one—informing me that one consignment of a 50 T mobile crane, which was recently ordered from HQ for our project was at the foothills and there was some problem faced by the transporter as the local citizens were creating issues and those two trailers were stuck up at the foothills after crossing the bad turns. He requested me to accompany the contractor who was a personal friend of our boss as the contractor was a retired Additional Chief Engineer and an ex-colleague of his, who after retirement was into the transportation business. He was a gentleman and reached my house after some time. The drivers of the trailers were stuck up in the trailer and there was also no food material with them.

I went out with them in their Gypsy to Merapani and saw that the people were coming with their luggage, cattle, and so many things and the crowd went on increasing as we proceeded. I understood that something serious had happened but we were going towards the foothills with ration for the four people stuck up in their trailer just above the foothills. However, the situation looked very grim. We reached the Merapani police outpost to understand what was happening and we were told that there was a border dispute between the two states and some firing did happen last night there. Nobody actually knew who had gotten shot. They advised us not to go but we had the responsibility to at least provide the food materials to the drivers who were coming from long distances. We decided to go slowly and saw a lot of people near the check gate with *Dao*'s and other weapons. We crossed the CRPF camp and reached our vehicles and just handed them the food materials. Suddenly, at that time, some firing happened again and we did not know exactly what was happening and who was firing whom. Within no time, there were huge gatherings of people on the Nagaland side, with all kinds of weapons on them. Our Gypsy driver was trembling. I told him to sit at the back and I came to the driver's seat. By any means, we had to cross the CRPF Camp.

Luckily, our vehicle was a Nagaland registered number plate and although people on the Nagaland side stopped our vehicle, seeing the vehicle registration and my fluent talking in Nagamese, they let us go. They advised us not to go to the Assam side as we could face problems. We thanked them but went down very slowly towards the CRPF camp as we understood that the number plate would create a problem on the Assam side. As expected, our vehicle was stopped just after crossing the gate by the mob on the Assam side. I talked to them very loudly and in our language and told them our identity. Luckily, no harm was made to us except for some damage to the back of our Gypsy. I have faced so many dangerous situations but it is always very risky to face a mob. After crossing the crowd, gradually we proceeded to Golaghat but along the whole road, we found people were fleeing with whatever they could carry with them. The transport contractors, who were sitting with me were in such a panic that I was worried about them but, at last, we reached Golaghat safely and the drivers of the trailers could stay there at least for a week as we had given them enough food and water for their stay in the vehicle itself.

Soon, both the governments met and resolved the issue at least temporarily and the trailers, after the delivery of the material, safely reached back to Golaghat.

UNIT 3 UNDERWATER PARTS ERECTION

During my absence, the RCE and my SE had taken a decision: to start the Unit 2 work of spiral casing with an absurd method.

In very simple terms, the water from the reservoir enters the water conductor system i.e. tunnel when the tunnel intake gate is opened and the stoplog lifted, (entry point to tunnel from reservoir) and water reaches the valve house through the tunnel. The gradient in the tunnel portion is not very sharp. The water through the tunnel reaches the valve house. When valve house gate is opened, water enters the penstock and reaches the Main inlet valve (MIV) of the Unit. Penstock is made of steel liner as the drop from valve house to Main Inlet valve is high and so the water pressure. The water than enters through MIV to the spiral casing when MIV is opened. The stay vane and stay rings is welded to the spiral casing and allows entry of water through stay vane which directs the water to the guide vane. The Guide   vane which controls the amount of the water entering and hit the runner of the turbine and as a reaction to the water pressure the turbine rotates. To increase or decrease of output, the guide vane will control the amount of water entering to the runner. After that the water goes out through the draft tube to the tail pool and then to the downstream of the river. The runner which is coupled with the turbine and generator shaft, rotates with water pressure as a reaction. After erection, the spiral is completely covered with concrete.

By this time, we had a 50 T mobile crane for the project. They had decided that by making some temporary arrangements (with a substantial cost), they would lower the Crane to the pit and lower the spiral segments down with the Crane at the pit. They did not think about how the crane would be taken out after the work; even with very basic engineering knowledge, that would have been an absurd idea. Bhupen was too junior to argue with the RCE and he told me this as soon as I arrived at the station. It seemed he was only waiting for me to stop the work like that. I was very surprised and very angry. BB told me to be in the powerhouse at nine am the next day while the RCE, the contractor, and my SE would also be there. At the site, the RCE told me his plan and to place a note for his approval. I point-blank told him "No" and he lost his temper. He and my SE were scolding me in the presence of all the officers and contractors. BB, being a civil Engineer, could not understand what the problem was and took me to a distance to know why I was objecting. I briefed him and he understood. I told him that we should focus on making the crane beam ready up to Unit 2 instead and if it could not be done, then we could try Unit 3 instead of Unit 2 from the opposite side with the mobile crane without lowering it. He told me to go ahead as I thought was right and he also told me that he would talk with the RCE on the matter. I thanked him for his understanding and that if the EOT crane beam was ready and a crane was in a position to move up to Unit 2, we could have done that. But the RCE had taken the matter personally and was not in talking terms with me for some time. Later, he understood and we went back to our cordial relationship.

Though I told BB that I will start from Unit 3, it was an extremely risky thing as the crane had to be placed in a very limited space as the hill started a few meters from Unit 3 and I also understood very well that if anything happened to the crane, I would lose my job. I called the crane operator and we were sitting in the space planning how to place the crane in the limited space and protect it from going down to the pit. The operator Bishen Singh told me that he would do it if I were with him. I told him that all of us would be with him and even in the case of any problem, I would take the full responsibility. He then confirmed that he would do it and take it as a challenge. Piku was also present as Bhupen had gone on leave. As planned, we stacked a lot of sandbags in front of the crane so that the front of the crane was in an elevated position than its back. After that, I called the contractor in charge of the civil work and asked him to pile at least five metres and put three 40 mm rods together in two places and fill with M 20 concrete. After a few days, with great effort and the expertise of Bishen Singh, our crane operator, we could successfully place the Crane in our desired location with its front in an upward position with respect to its back. We tied the back of the crane with those rods which were concreted with M-20 concrete. That was done only to make ourselves reassured so that we could lower the spiral segment down or not but the crane would not go down. The 8 T hydra mobile crane was used to bring the segments which were dimensionally quite big as Doyang was a low head machine but weight-wise around 4-5 T only. Bishon started his engine and released the boom length sufficient to, slung the first segment, the smallest one at first, and lowered it to the pit via a rail we placed earlier for lowering the segments sliding smoothly down. It was successful. Bishon was now fully confident that he could do it. One very senior OEM Engineer of the Bhopal plant, who was one of the best in machine Erection was very close to me and I had learned a lot about machine erection matters from him. He, at that time, was transferred to the commercial department at Bhopal itself and all the commercial issues of Doyang Units were looked after by him. His junior was there at that time in the project and was also a very competent Erection Engineer. He sat on the powerhouse site all day as all my officers were busy with this work and there was no one to attend to him in the office. He was observing with surprise what we were doing as it was not the normal practice of Erections. He, after going back to Bhopal, told his boss what I was doing here. I got a personal letter from him after some time, where he had written, "I understood what you were doing and the reason behind it and am very happy that you have accomplished it but as your elder brother, I advise you not to do this in future again." I treat this as the greatest recognition from a person who himself was a master in this field. One by one, we lowered all the segments and removed the crane without any problem. BB was very happy but the RCE and my SE were not so till the work was completed and congratulated us when we handed over the site to the civil wing for concreting. In the process, I did not incur any additional expenditure except for the food expenses for the staff who were continuously on the job and a small party after the work was arranged for them. The RCE's proposal had huge financial implications which we had avoided. After the welding of the segments and the radiography and ultrasonic test, Unit 3 was handed over for concreting of the barrel.

Unit 2 was deferred till the crane beam was made ready and my contractor's people were busy with Unit 3 for the next few months till the crane beam was extended up to Unit 2.

PROJECT PICNIC

Every year, a picnic was organised in the project centrally and one division would take the responsibility to organise the same every year in rotation. It became a tradition in the project. All the project employees and their families participated in it. In January 99', it was the turn of my division. So far, my division had grown manifold and three new Engineers had joined my division. Some *khalasis* or office staff and technical workmen had also joined. The contractor of the powerhouse and switchyard also mobilised their manpower fully. For the picnic, the local heavyweights were also invited by the organiser and normally they attended. We were very careful that not a single person of the local village leaders should be left out.

We planned to celebrate the same in a big way and the site was selected at an island (there are such islands created during the winter in the river which are submerged during summer). It was a beautiful place. But no vehicle except for a truck could reach there, crossing the water in the river at that time. I told the CE about our plan; he and his wife also had to go to the location on the truck and he was just thrilled to hear our plan. Accordingly, in the early morning, our people with all the required material reached the location before five am. All marketing was done in Golaghat the previous day. By seven in the morning, people started coming. Two trucks were ferrying them to the picnic spot from the other side of the river. My family was also at Doyang and they also joined. Breakfast with bread and butter and boiled egg and oranges were served with black tea. Soon, the atmosphere became very entertaining. Bhupen with his guitar and some of my staff with *Dhol* (local drum) and Bihu songs made the environment lovely. We put a few *shamianas* to save the people from direct sunlight and all those camps were soon filled with people. BB and the senior party started playing rummy at one such camp. Women were in another. Young boys were sitting in one and running from here and there to arrange everything to make the day memorable. Everyone was enjoying it. Drinks were also in abundance. People were enjoying their time. The lunch was ready: chicken, fish, mutton, and egg were all available. For vegetarians, paneer was specially made. After the children and the female batch finished eating, the male officers with the village leaders sat for lunch. At that time, our main local leader Charao Jami reached there. Charao had helped me a lot in some of the most difficult situations like during the transportation of heavy equipment. We were sitting for lunch and on my right were BB and the other senior officers. Charao was on my left. Rice was served and then dal and meat. Charao told me that he will not take chicken, etc. and he left with his usual *dao* to the river. Within 10 minutes, he came back with something in his hand. We were all waiting for him to join us for lunch. With his *dao*, he cut his catches into small pieces and put a lot of green chillies and salt over them. Then, he started eating his rice with his favourite salad prepared fresh by hand and finished his lunch. Seeing this, I started feeling very uncomfortable and I could not take my food. All were joking with me as if I were drunk but that day being the organiser, I had not taken a single drop but the scene was such that I could not eat anything. Everyone started dancing, singing, and playing some innovative games till the evening and had to be carried by the trucks to the other bank of the river in the evening. It was such a beautiful event except that I missed my lunch courtesy to Charro, my good friend.

During that time, I brought my family to be with me for some time. One evening, I was taking them to the powerhouse site in my Gypsy. I observed from a distance that colony 1 was in darkness. But on the other side, the power supply was there. I was just crossing gate 2, in front of the paramilitary camp. Suddenly, two gunmen from insurgent groups in army fatigue with firearms in their hands signalled me to stop. I stopped my Gypsy and came out. They checked the vehicle and then a senior man who was also fully armed came to me and said sorry and that they had by mistake stopped me as they were informed that some cadre of another militant group was moving in that area. I never told my family this side of the project stories; otherwise, I could have been forced to resign by my family long back. But now they had seen it and were shocked by this incident.

Everything was exposed and I had to tell my wife at least about some of the incidents. The big problem we faced was the local contractor's asking for petty work and fighting amongst themselves and they were creating havoc inside the project office. All Engineers were facing serious threats from those people. Even in the contractors' labour camps, they created a lot of problems. Once, there was a tender for hiring a vehicle for the OEM's project manager as we had to provide them with a vehicle as per contract. The tender was decided by our contract department and the work order was issued. Thereafter one evening, I was with my Engineer Khongwer in my office, discussing a drawing and the drawing was kept on the table to confirm certain technical matters. My intercom rang and our head of Finance called me and informed me that one local who participated in the tender and did not get a supply order for a vehicle had come to him and created a lot of problems, including the destruction of his office furniture. He told me that the person might also come to my office, so I should be careful. I just kept the phone on the receiver when a big-sized stone just went above my head as that man had already reached my office and had thrown the stone from near the entry point to my office. I was saved by an inch only. The HOF had already informed the CRPF, who was there at that time and they followed this miscreant and arrested him after a long chase. He was handed over to the local police. In the evening, I came to know that he was released by the police and my life was at risk. I left for Golaghat that night itself and came back after the intervention of the RCE with the DGP of the state. These types of incidents became very common and after the peace negotiation with the insurgents and the government, a ceasefire was declared in 1997. After the ceasefire project, the situation further deteriorated and all our Engineers and Contractors were suffering very badly. The cadres who were under command earlier and had some discipline before the ceasefire became hooligans and they entered the contractor labour camps and ate and destroyed their readymade food. These things were going on for nearly two years and later came under some control.

DEATH OF A CADRE

I was driving from the powerhouse with Bhupen next to me in my Gypsy at around one pm when we reached colony 1, gate no. 2. A fully armed person, who identified himself as the area commander of an outfit, stopped my vehicle and asked for some work to be given to him. I requested him to participate in the tender. He was quite decent in his talking and after the exchange of some courtesy talk, we left and went to our house for lunch. People like him were roaming inside the project freely without any hindrance even with the presence of all kinds of security forces. Unless we obeyed their request or orders, we were at their mercy and would have our lives at risk. No one could help us from physical harm. The RCE's incident was a lesson to us—that we had to safeguard ourselves without any external help. We completed our work as fast as possible and left the project. Therefore, the early project completion was our motto at that time. The contractors of the main work packages were the main sufferers and they were compelled to abide by all kinds of demands from these people.

At around 3:30 pm, we were returning to the powerhouse. We saw some people carrying a dead body fully covered in white cloth. I stopped my vehicle and asked who the person was and to my utter surprise, we were told that the commander whom we met an hour earlier was the person who died while bathing in the river near the gate by drowning. That was in winter and the river was almost dry, carrying the minimum amount of water only and people could not die from drowning at that location. Further, they were jungle fighters and very good swimmers, too. We understood that something else had happened. We proceeded to the powerhouse.

The commander of the security force and the newly joined Major of that area, who were stationed at colony 1 just in front of gate 2, invited me for a drink at his quarter the next night and gradually we became good friends. One benefit from the episode was that we were getting our drinks from the army canteen as Nagaland was a dry state and we got our scotch at a very cheap price.

SHIVA RATRI AT THE PROJECT

From my office, a road went up the hill and at the top of the hill, a Shiva Temple was made by our employees and was maintained by one Sri. Nath, an employee from the workshop division. People believed that all their wishes were fulfilled by visiting the place. This place was very calm and quiet and the Doyang river and the nearby hilltops could be seen from there. A very beautiful place indeed. Normally, when there was exhaustion or tiredness after a long day, I used to visit the place. When my family visited the project, I took them there. Nath took care of me and my family whenever I went there and he never forgot to offer me a cup of tea from his house nearby. I also used to visit his place. Nath was due to retire shortly and all his children were outside the state. He and his wife stayed there alone. Every year, during the Shiva Ratri festival, all the employees, contractors, workmen, and people from nearby places visited the temple. The whole day, there was a flow of people. The road from my office to the temple was nearly 300 m and was very steep and narrow. Only small vehicles could move on that road. On the Shiva Ratri day, all vehicles were to stop at the foothills and people had to walk that 300 m up the hill on foot.

It was in February, 2000 and Shiv Ratri was celebrated that year as well. Jeet, the Major, and I were there together with Bhaskar, who had recently joined my office. After offering Puja, Nath came running to us and requested us not to leave as he had prepared some special Prasad for us. After some time, he came to us with three glasses with something prepared from milk. We saw some green leaf sort of thing there and on asking, he told us that it was *Lord Shiv Baba's Prasad*. Bhaskar did not take it. It was very tasty and we thanked Nath for the Prasad and came down after sometime. By the time we reached down, I was experiencing something curious—I was feeling very light and I could not understand whether my legs were on the ground or not. I handed over the vehicle key to Bhaskar and told him to drive to my house as I was not in a position to drive. By the time I reached home, I was in a really bad shape and went straight to my bed. I could not sleep; I felt I was just going up, up and up flying. Seeing my condition, Bhaskar called Dr. Dutta who came immediately. He was very worried as my BP also rose very steeply. In the meantime, Jeet and the Major also complained of the same problem. All three of us seemed to have a serious health conditions. The doctor went straight to the hospital and came back within 10-15 minutes. During that time, I was mischievously behaving with all nearby. Knowing my condition, a lot of people reached my house. The doctor came back and requested me to lie down, which I vehemently resisted. Ultimately, with help of the people in my house, he was successful to give me two injections. After a few minutes, I felt very sleepy and went to bed. I slept for more than eight to nine hours and when I opened my eyes, I saw a lot of people, including BB standing in front of me. I gradually recollected what had happened. I felt so ashamed but felt very thirsty and hungry. Dr. Dutta came to me and told me that my condition was very precarious at that time and my BP crossed 200 plus, which he was constantly monitoring even when I was fully asleep. Everyone had a sigh of relief to see me coming back to normalcy. I came to know that Jeet and the Major also had the same problem and treatment. The doctor was running to take care of all three of us. By the grace of God, all three of us recovered. From that day itself, I promised myself not to touch such things in future and I kept that promise to date.

SWITCHYARD CHARGING

One of the major mistakes probably made by our designer was to have three-phase generator transformers for the units without considering the transportation bottlenecks. Though they were transported in Nitrogen filled condition to lower the transportation weight and to remove all bushings and accessories, their height and weight was a major challenge. By that time, the road was a bit improved by cutting the sharp bends but the height of the transformer above the trailer would touch the 33 kV lines in two locations on the road. We had taken permission from the Nagaland power department where our RCE was the boss once and we got the permission to dismantle the lines every time we brought those three transformers by our team and re-erected the lines as soon as the trailer crossed those sections. Every time, we faced serious resistance from the citizens of the area even for a shutdown of the line even if it was less than two hours.

The generation of the Doyang project was designed to transmit its power to Dimapur by a double circuit 132kv line and to Mokakchaung and Kohima through single circuit lines. It has a five MVA 132/33 station supply bay in addition to three incoming unit bays and a bus coupler bay. As such, it was a reasonably big switchyard. The switchyard was ready by the middle of 1999 and we planned to back charge it from Dimapur Powergrid End substation to keep the switchyard charged before commissioning the Units and to have a Grid power supply to the project and colony to avoid Diesel powerhouse supply as soon as possible. The charging of the switchyard was a priority. But unfortunately, we had a contractor who had to be pushed daily for progress and ultimately Dimapur Bays were ready for charging without PLCC (Power line carrier Communication) and PLCC panels were to be delayed and we could not wait. As such, there was no direct communication with Dimapur from DHEP.

The problem of communication with Dimapur in the absence of a telephone network or PLCC (power line carrier communication) was critical. Peculiar problems needed peculiar handling. We had decided to go ahead with a very interesting communication arrangement. Bhupen and I, with one Engineer from the contractor, were the only persons available on the date of charging in the SY. I put one of my Engineers at our WT station. Communication from SY and Doyang WT station at the permanent colony was through our intercom connections. Doyang WT station was contacting our WT station at Shillong, where I kept one HQ Engineer to receive the message from Doyang WT station. After receiving the message, he communicated with Dimapur via telephone and the same process was adopted for the return messages. With the development of the 4G communication system as of now, this might look like a story in the present-day world but we had to work with those limitations. I always tell my juniors that if you have the will to do something, the limitations can be overcome without much difficulty. Some solutions will come out from somewhere. I still remember when my three Engineers and I, after several hours of discussion at the site, could not find out a solution to a problem but suddenly a workman came and asked a question to me without knowing anything about what we were discussing; all of us were looking at each other in surprise as that was the solution we did not even think of. I always listen to everyone's suggestions and consult with almost everyone concerned before making a decision, which may sometimes go wrong but once a decision was made, I could not tolerate if someone violated it as if it weren't the team's decision. I have told this to all my team members repeatedly and clearly. People cannot be hundred percent right but decisions cannot be kept pending. My earlier boss DPD had taught me the lesson and I earnestly followed his advice, which was always very true.

Everything was going fine and around three pm, we had given clearance to charge the Dimapur-Doyang Ckt I through the communication arrangement we had made. We did not know exactly when the message had reached Dimapur by the Powergrid Engineers. Suddenly, we heard the hissing sound of the Line charging and immediately thereafter a lightning arrestor got burned and the line tripped to our utter disappointment. We had taken a formal shut down and communicated to Dimapur via the same communication arrangement. It was almost half an hour later that we got the confirmation message from Dimapur. Bhupen told me, "Rajat da, forget about it today, we will try some other day," but I decided to go for the second attempt after changing the damaged LA.

We reached the store but the Crane driver was not available. I took the key and decided to operate the crane myself and Bhupen assisted me. As no other help was available at that hour of the day, it was around 6:30 pm and in Nagaland people used to go to bed very early.

We took out a spare LA from the store and Bhupen, Mr. Singh, an Engineer from the contractor, and I properly slung the LA to the 8T Hydra crane for transporting it to the switchyard, which was nearly a kilometre from the store. I found the crane brake in very bad shape and for braking, one had to stand on the brake to stop. The road from the stores to SY was a sharp gradient down for around 300 m and then had an upward gradient to reach the SY. We were a bit worried but I was so determined to charge the SY that evening and we started towards SY. Bhupen and Singh helped me to carry the spare LA by the 8 T Hydra crane, which was not less than 15 years old and was shifted from the Kopili project long back and did not properly respond to our commands. However, by God's grace, we reached safely at the SY with the LA.

The damaged LA was removed and the new one was placed. By that time, it was 9:30 pm. The Engineer in Shillong wanted to go home but I requested him to wait. After we were ready, we again gave charging clearance through the same communication channel and closed the circuit breaker manually at around10:30 pm. We heard the hissing sound of the line being charged. The line charging was successful this time. We waited there for some time and found everything to be normal. Bhupen and I went to the powerhouse and found the panels/meters were all working fine. At eleven pm, we informed Dimapur via Shillong to take shut down as all parameters were found okay. We thanked our Engineer at Shillong for his cooperation and all were very happy.

My vehicle, the Gypsy which was ambushed during the attack on security forces at the time of my joining there, was repaired and was later allotted to me. Bhupen and I used that vehicle and since we had no working hours, the driver was used only when we went out of the project or for filling of the petrol, cleaning, etc. We drove ourselves within the project. Bhupen, from his pocket, put a music system in the vehicle. The vehicle was used by both of us. The drivers were very happy to work with us as they remained free all day except when we went out of the project.

From PH, we started to our quarter. It was twelve past midnight. Bhupen was driving. Suddenly near colony 2, he stopped the vehicle and put the tape at full blast. Fast and dancing songs, hits of that time, came out at midnight in the middle of the road at full volume. I also came down spontaneously and we were dancing on the road. It was simply madness at the midnight. Maybe, we were dancing for quite some time before realising that we had not taken anything since breakfast and suddenly our tummy started giving warnings to us with all kinds of sounds. The first milestone of the project was achieved and we were happy in achieving something too dear to us under the most difficult situation. The enjoyment we got with this success and our spontaneous celebration at midnight cannot be compared with any appreciation letter or cash awards. It comes from our hearts when we do something with all our efforts and become successful, then naturally, the enjoyment comes from the heart and there is no substitute for this pleasure. I still remember sometimes the way we communicated and took the risk of charging. Today, I will not allow my juniors to take such risks. Communication at present days is so improved that people will not believe also that some crazy people like us work with such limitations and madness only due to the sheer interest in doing something to be proud of later. I agree with the following famous quote by Aswath Damodaran and try to follow that in my life:

"Risk pervades our daily life. Without taking risks we cannot progress, every major advance in human civilization, from caveman's invention of tools to gene therapy has been made possible because someone was willing to take a risk and challenge the status quo."

We reached home past one am. Deepak was waiting for us. Seeing us, he immediately warmed the food already cooked for us. I needed a bath badly so I decided to take a bath before dinner. Bhupen was shouting to me from outside to come out of the bath early as he was very hungry and could not wait with food in front. After having food, Bhupen told me that since this was the first activity of the project commissioning, we must inform the CE at night itself as he was so helpful to all our efforts and we went to BB's house that night and woke him up. First, he was very worried and asked if anything had happened, which was almost common in those days. Without taking much time, we explained to him what had happened. He was very happy and promised us a party shortly. Some senior officials were aloof from what was going on and so we decided not to disturb them at night and let them know all about it the next day.

The next day, I got up around 10 am when Bhupen shouted. Deepak was quick to serve us breakfast with Lucchi, aloo dum, and egg. We found it very delicious. We went to meet the SE in his office to brief him on the whole story from yesterday and told him that we would keep the SY charged from that day and were planning to charge the Station service transformer so that colony supply can be made from Grid power instead of Diesel power supply. Engineers were required to be put on shift and some engineers from Diesel powerhouse were shifted to the powerhouse shift duty.

We also met the RCE and BB and invited them to the SY in the afternoon to have a cup of tea together with my whole team. We moved straight to SY and decided to keep the SY charged during the visit of the CE and RCE in the evening. The transformer oil filtration and other pre-commissioning test results were excellent and could be charged at any time. We decided that at least one colony feeder will be charged that day if the transformer charging passed off successfully.

With the same communication strategy, we charged the SY at around one pm without any problem. Deepak in the meantime sent us our lunch to SY through our driver Lokho.

We were taking our lunch and planning to charge the transformer at no load from the 132 kV side as all pre-commissioning checks results were fine. That day, enough labour was arranged from our contractor and also some from other contractors and we had no problem related to manpower that day.

Around three pm, we charged the station service transformer 132/33 kV and the transformer behaved perfectly. All the senior officers of the project reached the SY site. They were very happy and congratulated us for achieving the first milestone of the project commissioning.

We had a small tea party there. Everyone, especially, Bhupen and I were very relaxed after the successful charging of the transformer. We deferred our decision to charge the colony line to the next day and left the SY and the Transformer remained charged continuously from then and the shift duty started from that day at the powerhouse control room. Soon we were able to commission the PLCC, which was delayed very long due to the malfunction of some of its components whose replacements were to come from Mumbai. Doyang-Dimapur communication now became much easier.

We were very tired and decided to go back home early. While returning, we met the Major on the road. We shared the news with him and he told us he would be reaching my quarter after some time. We had just finished our tea when the Major with two or three sepoys reached my house with chicken and two full bottles of special scotch. The sepoys removed Deepak from the kitchen and started preparing various starters and chicken by themselves, which they brought with them in army style. The party was going on for quite a long time till midnight and Jeet and Tilak also joined. When we finished, the meal was served. Bhupen was a teetotaller and we had finished the bottles the Major had arranged. Bhupen was busy with the snacks and repeatedly told us to stop as he was very hungry.

The Major left after midnight and Bhupen also left after dinner. I went to bed very tired after all the tensions of SY charging. The brake of the crane made my feet hurt. The next day, we extended the grid power supply to the colony. For the first time, colony people could get proper voltage in their houses and the DG powerhouse people got some rest.

One day, I was in the powerhouse service bay supervising a major activity of rotor lowering from the service bay. All were given different responsibilities and one man was above the rotor assembly to give signal to the crane operator at the top as it was to be lowered inch by inch. The rotor assembly that was more than 100 T was to be placed within the stator assembly already placed in the locations. The gap between stator and rotor was 12 mm only. It was a very precise operation.

At that time, one bus full of villagers came in and their leader gave me a letter from the Deputy commissioner, requesting us to allow the villagers to see the powerhouse. I sent them down with one of my Engineers and kept myself engaged on the job. Suddenly, I heard somebody talking behind me in Nagamese, "This is possible only by the Indians and only they can do this." Few old people in the group who did not go down were talking amongst themselves. I realised that the insurgents had made these innocent villagers understand that they are not a part of India. After my work was done successfully, I had a very frank talk with them and told them that we are as human as they are and I showed my local Engineers to them and explained that they are the backbone of the project and capable of doing such things. They were grateful to me and blessed us all in their language which I did not understand.

OCCUPATION OF THE QUARTERS

The project activities were going on at full speed and we now had no working hours. We were running with time to achieve the milestone. To relax in between, a few of us kept ourselves busy on the badminton court in the evenings and went to the powerhouse to supervise the night shifts. Deepak and Bhaity were engaged on a temporary basis called "master roll." Sabin who replaced Deepak and Bhaity stayed in my house and he sometimes made pakoras and tea for the players. Life suddenly became too hectic. The erection team was busy all the time. Normally, the senior officials were comparatively relaxed. The RCE, the old man of the Project, reduced his stay in the project and BB now normally looked after the project work.

One day among the Senior officers, only Pranab and I were in the station and all others were out of the project for various reasons.

I reached home from the work site around nine pm and went straight to the badminton court. Pranab was waiting for me. We were playing badminton and it was around 9:30 pm. Our quarters were at the top of the hill from where all areas of the project were partially visible. Suddenly, we heard gunshots exchanged near the Dam site and gunfire in the night's darkness was visible. It was continuing the whole night and we were all very scared. We contacted the security camp but we were not getting any proper reply. We told Sabin, who had replaced Deepak and Bhaity, to serve our dinner. After the meal, we heard the gunfire going on till around two o' clock intermittently and then there was a lull. It was three o' clock at night when we went to our bed without knowing what had happened.

Cling, cling, cling.

I got up with the most disgusting sound of the intercom phone. It was around seven in the morning and on the other side of the line was the officer in charge of the Doyang police station.

"May I talk to the powerhouse Engineer?"

I asked who he was.

He told me that he was the officer in charge of the police station and informed me that there was an exchange of fire between two factions of the underground groups and there was one dead body lying just outside the project boundary. He requested for a truck to pick up the dead body and to send it to Wokha, the district HQ town for post mortem.

I told him that the truck driver stays at colony 3 and the key remained with him. He could take the truck with the driver named Sema. The OC was very thankful. I observed he was very terrified by the incident.

He rang me again after an hour to tell me that Sema could not be located and most of the project people had already fled either to Golaghat or Wokha with whatever communication they got.

The project work came to a total standstill again. I was very worried and went to Pranab's room to discuss what to do as we two were the senior Engineers present in the project on that day. We went to the police station, after failing to locate any driver. All were simply missing. We were waiting, thinking about what to do and at that time, a dumper was coming from the quarry site which belonged to the Dam construction company. The driver, not knowing about what had happened in the project last night, stopped his dumper at our signal and it was around 11 am.

We all went to the incident site with the dumper and the OC arranged to pick up the dead body in the dumper and we reached back to the PS around two pm. After doing the required formalities, the OC sent the body to Wokha with a police escort for post mortem. The OC was very grateful to us and went on continuously thanking us. We came back home straight away as we were feeling very hungry and a bath was an urgent requirement. All of us were sweating even on the winter days.

I had a good bath and Sabin arranged lunch for us. Without losing any time, I went to my bed after lunch so that I could sleep for some time. I was just lying in my bed when suddenly there was a knock on my bedroom door. Sabin or Pranab or any of my colleagues never knocked before entering and they came straightway with a song or some kind of shouting. I was surprised and worried and came to the door. The door was just closed and not locked as usual. I opened the door and found two people in Army fatigue fully armed and standing in front of my bedroom door and a gentleman was just behind them. Seeing me, he came forward and extended his hand for a handshake. With a smile, he introduced himself. I got the shock of my life as his name was known to me and for all the wrong reasons.

I was about to come out but he stopped me and told me about the incident that happened the day before and that they had a major fight with some other group and were worried that more such incidents in retaliation may happen today. They had also mobilised their full strength and since our house was at the hilltop, their cadre had already occupied my other room. I came out to see the other room to find that the room was already occupied by nearly 20-25 people all armed and they were making their beds on the floor. My kitchen was also occupied by their people. The gentleman was making excuses as to why he had to act fast and so he had occupied my house without any intimations, forgetting about permission. Even if he had given us some information also, we could have done nothing at all. Those were happening in the presence of all the security forces in the area unchallenged. I went to Pranab's quarter only to find the same situation except that his kitchen was left unoccupied. These people had come in a few vehicles from colony 2 side after crossing all security forces placed for our protection without facing any resistance and later, we came to know that it was because the cease-fire was going on, they were unable to act. The security could do nothing but become spectators in the whole drama. We were to care of our lives by ourselves only and complete the project. I came back to my bedroom. Sabin came in after some time and his face looked as if he was going to vomit. He told me that they were preparing beef in my kitchen. Even in this grave situation, a smile came to my face and I felt so sorry for Sabin.

I had just come out of my bedroom again when I noticed that the boys were already settled down in the other room. Seeing me, a few started talking in Nagamese, which I had already been comfortable with. Some showed how the firearm worked and I was very worried that something might go wrong accidentally. Then, one Senior cadre called a boy and introduced him to me as the hero of last night who had killed the person and as a reward, the dead man's gun was presented to him by his commander. I went to Pranab and with Sabin, we left our house as staying there would be a nightmare. With few essentials, we reached the guest house. We noticed that searchlight was used by these people and full patrolling by the cadres was going on from the evening in presence of all the forces present in the locality.

The next day we sent one officer to Golaghat to contact BB who was in Guwahati and to also inform the HQ. A message was also sent to the RCE.

In the guest house, after having dinner, we went on talking and discussing our plans. Sleep was not possible. Maybe, late at night sleep overtook me and I was in bed till nine o' clock the next morning. None disturbed me. Most of the guest house staff had already fled. Getting a cup of tea and breakfast on time also became very difficult and Sabin made tea and breakfast for us at the guest house.

By 11 am, we left for the powerhouse and other sites and spent time with our Engineers and the support staff. They were fully demoralised and after we reached there, they felt good; they felt that at least there was someone still with them to take care of them. Most people did not know what had happened and that was why it had become more panicky. We explained to them the situation. What had happened had already happened and we were not the target for all these incidents, we told them.

We came to the guest house and had our lunch by three pm. Sabin informed us that all those people were still there and could not be expected to vacate our quarters shortly. We were waiting for our seniors to come on the one hand and on the other hand, we did not want them to be back for their safety. After a few days, BB and other senior officers reached Golaghat and called us to Golaghat. Unfortunately, there was heavy rain at night and there were a lot of landslides on the road up to the foothills. We started. Driver Lokho took shovels, etc. with him and we took a four-wheeler vehicle. We reached Bagti but after that, the road was damaged. Before reaching Bhandari, it seemed that the whole hill had come down and there was no possibility that the vehicle could pass. We left our shoes in the jeep and started walking, negotiating with knee-deep mud. After around two km of walking, which took us more than three hours, we reached a better portion of the road and from there, the office of the Bhandari Sub-divisional officer was around two km. We reached there fully exhausted. Seeing our condition, the officer offered us coffee with snacks and he arranged our dropping at the Merapani Sarmah tea stall. Sarmah arranged an ambassador car on rent for us to go up to Golaghat. In the meantime, we took our favourite Paratha and Jalebi and became fresh for our next journey to Golaghat. By the time we reached Golaghat, it had already become dark.

After some time, the RCE also reached Golaghat from Kohima via Dimapur. We were explaining to all the senior officials what had happened in the last few days and that our quarters were still under occupation. Everyone was so tense and no one opened their mouths for some time. Ultimately, it was decided that the RCE and BB would go to Shillong to brief the top management. They all told us to take a break for some time and others were going back to the project after the opening of the road. It was quite late at night when I reached home. All were surprised to see me at that hour of the night and I was also very tired and exhausted. I told them that everything was alright and I was late only because of the road and vehicle problem. If they knew the actual story, I could have been forced to resign.

I was with my family for a week. My twin babies were now around six months and my mother and my mother-in-law helped my wife to take care of them. My daughter was only a bit more than four years old, so she also needed constant care, otherwise, she would feel neglected. But at only four, she was so mature that she started taking care of herself and helped her mother to take care of her brothers. Looking back now, in the name of the Project, I was missing those beautiful parts of my life very badly. I sometimes regret my inability to be with my family at those times as I was so involved in the project and it seemed commissioning of the machine got more priority than my own family. One night, my elder son was not well and suddenly his temperature became too high and he was almost senseless. My mother put a spoon in between his jaws and I talked to the doctor, a friend of mine. He gave him an injection and after some time, the temperature gradually came down. The doctor told me that some kids had this problem and their body temperature suddenly rose, which made them senseless. He advised me to keep the drug

Fabrilix with me always and in such cases to feed him immediately without waiting for the doctor. My son had that problem till he was around five years old and Fabrilix was always available in my house. Because of the communication issues, when once my family was admitted to hospital for some food poisoning type of issue and because the Merapani road was closed due to a heavy landslide, I received the information after four days and by the time I was there, they were all discharged from the hospital.

After nearly a week, I came to know that my house was vacated by those unauthorised people and cleaning was also done properly by the building division. I was very worried about leaving for the project even though my son was fully fit by then. I requested the doctor for his help and I am so grateful to him that later also in such emergencies, he immediately visited on receipt of the phone call from my wife.

I left for the project.

The project was gradually coming back to normalcy and all the site started functioning, of course, not to the full strength. The labourers who fled were gradually coming back. In general terms, the situation was tense but under control and the project and activities were limping back.

After coming back, I could not concentrate on my work for some days. I was still in shock from the incident that had happened. The sickness of my kid kept my mind busy as I couldn't do anything from there as well as no communication with home was possible. We were regularly in touch with the BSNL authorities for telephone connections but without any success. Unlike the present days, no other service provider was in existence and BSNL had the monopoly.

A few days later, BB called me to his chamber. He handed me a cheque for Rs. 2500 and I was surprised at what had happened. Then, he laughed and told me it was the CEO's instruction to pay me this amount to change my utensils. We enjoyed the fact that at least the HQ officials thought (I know, it was only one person but who cares) about their employees in the remotest places. I accepted the cheque with gratitude. I had already changed all my utensils and bought them new from Golaghat before returning to the project.

FLOODING OF THE POWERHOUSE

It was a bright sunny morning. The switchyard was energised recently and we were waiting for the readiness of the Dam to commission Unit I of the power station. Not much work in the powerhouse was left for the Unit I; the pre-commissioning tests were already done and we were waiting for the filling up of the tunnel for Unit 1.

Bhupen and I reached the switchyard in the morning and it was a bright sunny day. We were in a very relaxed mood and just moving around there. We were looking at the powerhouse from the switchyard, which was at an elevation much above the powerhouse.

Suddenly, one workman started shouting that the river started flowing in the reverse direction and was coming towards the powerhouse building. We could not understand what he was saying and we ran to see what was happening. The worst had occurred. There was a big landslide just 100 m downstream of the diversion tunnel outlet that blocked the river flow and water had started flowing towards the powerhouse at a very high velocity. For a few minutes, Bhupen and I were dumbfounded but immediately we regained our senses. We cut the Breaker manually, stopping the total power supply to the powerhouse to avoid any mishap and rushed to the powerhouse. We ran down to the second floor, the Control room floor, to see if anything could be saved but the water level inside the powerhouse was rising very fast. We evacuated all our workforce from the powerhouse and luckily there was no casualty.

The whole powerhouse had gone underwater up to the control room floor. Unit 1, which was ready for commissioning, had gone underwater. Except for the Generator Transformer, the EOT crane, and the generator assembly of Unit 3, which was going on in the service bay, all others were going underwater.

Tears came to my eyes without stopping. All were waiting speechless in the service bay area. Senior Engineers had reached the site including BB, SE R&B, SE Dam and Spillway, and my SE. Everything was over by then. The tail pool was filled with turbine oil-filled water till service bay level. Only two or three days back, we had filled oil in the Turbine bearings to make the machine ready. Everything was gone. It was so heart-breaking.

We were all discussing what to do then. Pumping out the water from the powerhouse pit was meaningless unless the block in the river path was excavated and allowed the river to flow in its normal channel. Suddenly, we found my SE jumping in the Tail pool for swimming. Senior officials were so annoyed and all kinds of filthy comments followed.

Everyone was mentally depressed and BB told all of us to go home and meet at the PH site the next morning. Accordingly, we all dispersed.

The next morning, we assembled there. The normalisation of the river flow was the first step and accordingly, a team was constituted to start the work. The contractor for Dam Construction had provided all earth cutting equipment and manpower for this work.

Parallelly, I also started mobilising all the pump sets available with us and hired a few from Golaghat so that as soon as the river flow was normalised, we could start pumping out the water from the powerhouse. It took around seven to eight days to clear the river and water started flowing in its course. A small earthen dam was made near the tail pool so that pumped water did not backflow to the powerhouse building. With all these arrangements made, we started pumping out the water with six various capacity pumps from the tail pool discharging the water to the river. After a few days, the water was discharged from the third floor of the building. The water reached the top of the third floor where the control room was. The water level mark was visible on the walls of the control room. Though the water was discharged, the floor was under knee-deep mud. All control panels of all the Units were installed and all were under mud and not usable. Removing the mud was a major challenge. While Unit side mud could be handled with the help of the EOT crane with a bucket carrying mud, on the control room floor, all the removal work had to be done manually. There was a foul smell everywhere. We continued pumping water to the bottom floor level and allowed the mud to dry for a few days. We started from the Unit side. Unit I, which was ready for commissioning, was underwater and except for the underwater parts and the turbine, all the electrical systems like the total generator were under muddy water and required to be cleaned and treated to make it ready again for high voltage test. Luckily, for the other two units, the generator assemblies were at the service bay where pre-assembly was going on and, therefore, those were not affected by the flood but the control panels of all the three units were gone.

The top bosses from HQ came and it was decided to give replacement orders to the original suppliers without going through the tendering process for shortening the recommissioning schedule. This was a decision which we all were proud of as it helped us to get the material at the site quite faster. Because a delay of one day in commissioning meant a substantial amount of revenue loss as well.

The mud removal process seemed to become a never-ending process as there was a shortage of workmen for such jobs and foul smell discouraged people from going inside, making it impossible to work for a long time even with a mask. It took nearly 20 days before we could finally clear the mud and other debris and the building was washed with a high-velocity water jet. This had made the smell bearable and we gradually started dismantling the already erected but damaged equipment to the store for inspections by our underwriters later. Testing had no meaning for electronic equipment, which was under muddy water for such a long time. Those were then shifted to the stores for making the insurance claims. The stator and rotor were repairable and action was taken accordingly. Photographs were taken on all the steps. Unfortunately, those black and white photographs are all damaged now as they were not properly stored.

We started concentrating on Units 2 and 3 that were now ready for erection after cleaning the debris. Unit 3 turbine erection was already completed and generator assembly was at the service bay. The Unit 2 turbine erection was half done at the time of the flooding and generator assembly was yet to be started. We started the balance work of Unit 3 generator assembly. The stator was lowered smoothly from the service bay. The work was completed and the HV test was done without any problem. The Rotor assembly was going on in the service bay, which was almost ready for lowering.

We had lowered the turbine shaft. Since Doyang was a low-speed and bottom bracket supported machine, the erection was a bit easier than the Kopili Machines.

Within a short time, all the three machine erections were completed and by this time, the new panels also started coming. We got very busy and there was no work timing followed. Erection work was going on in three shifts. I had intentionally given work to one Engineer for the generator and shifted him to the turbine in the second machine and control system to him in the third unit, keeping the future maintenance concern in my mind. Similar arrangement was done for the other two engineers. Now, I got three Engineers, at least who knew the complete machine and could independently handle it. This decision helped me later during the operation and maintenance phase as all three were fully competent to look after all the systems of the machine and if anyone was not available, the other could take over his job. Similar action was taken with our Junior Engineers as well.

As soon as the machines were ready, the Dam was also ready and we inspected the tunnel, which was not very long and gave clearance for filling. The procedure was explained to all step-by-step. The tunnel filling process was started. During that time, few Junior Engineers were posted and all were local recruitment and they were fresh out of college. I had started to train them every evening by taking a class using the blackboard and giving them assignments under the supervision of an Engineer and teaching them with the actual machine to make them ready for operational work.

COMMISSIONING OF THE POWERHOUSE

All three units were put on spinning at a lower speed and were inspected. There were some minor problems and soon we could commission all the three units and put them on full load. This was the first central sector power project commissioned and to date it is performing exceptionally well in the state of Nagaland. I was very proud to lead a team of young Engineers without having any previous experience and to complete this project within the five years, even after the submergence of one unit and the control panels of all the Units. Furthermore, there were all kinds of non-technical problems as well as law-and-order issues. But everyone worked on a mission without having any modern types of equipment with threat to their life at all times. The BSNL also gave a connection to the project and after the joining of a very dynamic General Manager at Dimapur, our project came under his jurisdiction. I met him several times to explain to him our problems and he took action. However, most of the time, the line remained dead.

With the commissioning of all the units, we were much relieved. My daughter was very sick and the doctor at Golaghat advised an operation on her tonsil at the earliest. But I could not go out because of the commissioning activities going on in full swing and so I told my wife that I will be free shortly and would make a decision. But the doctor made her scared. After commissioning and observing the machine for a few days, I applied for leave and went to Guwahati. But the views of the doctor at Golaghat and Guwahati were totally different; therefore, we decided to go to Vellore Christian Medical College, leaving our twins with their grandmothers. In Vellore, they specifically told us that there was no need for any operation and sent us back with a nasal spray as they had diagnosed it as sinusitis and resulting mouth breathing that infected her adenoids glands to enlarge.

A big relief. We were very angry with our ENT doctor at Golaghat. They scared patients because of their ignorance.

After coming back, I returned to the project. Gradually, Engineers from the project were transferred but my name was not coming. The CEO was planning to make me the project head though at my rank, I was not eligible to be given those responsibilities but they were not getting anyone ready to come to head this project. I was much younger and I objected to it. None wanted to continue in such a situation in the project and the management had earlier assured us that they would transfer us to a better location after commissioning. But almost six months had gone by and I was waiting for the order, while most of my colleagues got their orders.

In November that year, we had taken normal shutdown of all the units for inspections and the main inlet valve was closed. Dewatering started from the tail pool with a few pumps, creating a small dam on the downstream side of the tail pool so that water after pumping out was not coming back. I found that a lot of villagers came there to catch fish. They waited with lanterns the whole night, but there was not a single fish. I told the security agency very strictly not to allow anyone to go to the tail pool as there was a risk of life because the tail pool water was quite deep. Overnight pumping lowered the tail pool water level and I told Piku, my Engineer in charge of dewatering, to drop the tail pool gate of all the units and to go on pumping out the water. In the morning, we entered the draft tube from the inspection manhole to find that it was full of fish. In all the units, it was the same story. We distributed the fish to all the villagers and our officials. I still remember the scene as I had never seen such a scene before: fish, large and small, had filled the draft tube.

Later, Doyang reservoir became a big source of income for the villagers as a huge quantity of fish was there and a lot of villagers started making fishing their livelihood. Various breeds of birds started coming there and the location soon became famous for Amar Falcon, which was coming in thousands in the winter months and it soon became a place of tourist attraction.

One evening, the manager of the local state bank and I were having dinner at the guest house as my cook was not there. We were very relaxed and both of us went to my house and were in my adjacent room, which I used as the guest room. Suddenly, someone attacked my house with big stones and my bedroom was fully damaged with all the glass windows broken to pieces and there were a lot of stones entering my bedroom. Luckily, I was not in my bedroom. Hearing this, all my friends and colleagues came, including our security people but they could not find anybody. At that time, BB was not in the station and my SE was in charge. I informed him and requested that the security personnel attached to the RCE must be instructed to be on mobile duty protecting the area as the RCE nowadays did not stay in the project for long and came once or twice a month for a few days. He did not come that night. The next day, I was surprised to see an order shifting the security people of the RCE's residence to the dam site instead of being put on mobile duty in our area as requested. I was very annoyed and got wild. I went to him and dropped my earned leave application to him. I told him that I would not come back to the project after the completion of my leave also, and if required, I would submit my resignation. I was sending extensions of my leave as soon as the earlier leave expired and did not come back. I went to Guwahati and met BB in our Guwahati office and submitted my request letter for transfer to him. He was not willing but after a lot of discussions, he finally agreed to forward the same to ED Project but later I came to know that he told the ED Project not to transfer me verbally. I went to meet ED Project who kept me waiting for a very long time and my anger gradually went up. I entered his room without waiting for permission and gave him the letter with the recommendation of BB. He refused to forward it to the Director. By this time, I lost all my patience and talked to him very badly and my voice was not courteous at all. My ex-CEO, during whose tenure my name was always deleted from the foreign training in Japan and Europe, was also sitting in his room and he was saying in between that I should not be removed from there as there would be no one who can handle the project. His comment made me mad. After seeing my temper and as I had already created a scene, he was scared. I know I am normally a very polite and decent person but when someone intentionally tries to harm me, provided I am right, I cannot control myself. I could not think of any more harm that he could do to me. I always prepared myself for the worst and for people with my level of experience and dedication, it was not difficult to get a job offered by some big companies with a steep hike in salary. ED (Project) must be scared with the raged face of mine and without speaking any further, he recommended. With this letter, I went to Shillong to the Director's office for approval of my transfer. The CEO was in Delhi at that time and for the transfer of our rank officers, the CEO's approval was necessary. The Director was a very scared person and he had some incident earlier with me in Kopili and he knew my character quite well. ED (Project) who was very close to the Director must have told him what had happened the earlier day with him. Without any delay, he recommended it. I sent the same to Delhi by fax and requested our Delhi office in charge to get the approval of the CEO. He was a very helpful person and he got the CEO's approval and finally, my transfer order to Shillong was released. I was to report to the ED commercial, who was a very nice gentleman.

I came back to Golaghat and sent a message to my SE for my release order as I did not want to go back there as I had told him before I came out of the project that I would not come to the Project again. BB sent me a personal letter, requesting me to be in the project for a formal farewell as he did not want to release me without a formal get together considering my contribution to the project. I went to the project and that evening BB arranged a grand farewell dinner for me where all the divisional Engineers were present and the next morning, I got my release order. I thanked BB and all my colleagues and left for Golaghat.

SECOND TIME IN SHILLONG

SHILLONG CALLED ME AGAIN

As per the transfer order, I left for Shillong. One of my colleagues was transferred out of Shillong and I was lucky to get his house in Motinagar, which was vacated by him. Our office was shifted to our permanent complex at the lower new colony and was quite far from my rented house. We did not have an official quarter available and instead, a house rent allowance was given to us. My house was on a hill slope and was on the ground floor of a two-storied building that had two parts; the other one was occupied by one of our HR officers. The front entrance was at our ground level but I had to park my car on the roof of the second floor coming from a different road. There were many small units on the campus and all were put on rent. A few beautiful dogs of the owner roamed around the area and one of them became very friendly with me. He stayed most of the time with me when I was there and he became very good company for me.

I joined the office of the Executive Director (Commercial) at that time called Corporate Economics. The fertile brain of a CEO in charge then who was also the Director (Finance) had contributed to the organisation by changing the names of a few establishments. Instead of doing something great for the company, he was busy changing names of the departments. The planning department was replaced as Corporate Futuristic like that and all funny ideas but no groundwork for future expansion or welfare of the employees was taken up during his tenure. My ED was a perfect gentleman. There were already two senior managers in the office and the ED had a problem with the allotment of work as none of the existing senior managers were prepared to leave some part of the work to be taken out from them and given to me. The ED was also so polite that he could not exercise his authority. I was practically without any work. When I met the boss for work allotment, he simply said, "You have done very hard work for so many years, so relax for some time." But I knew the actual reasons. When I went to him asking for leave, he became very happy that he would not require to face me for some time at least. That time, I had bought a piece of land at Golaghat and the Bank loan was also sanctioned. I started the construction of my house as there was no difficulty in getting the leave. The ED never asked me why I delayed or if I overstayed on my leave. It went on like that for a year and my house was almost ready and my family shifted there. As I was not given any work and leave was not an issue, I had given my energy to make my house during the period instead of sitting idle in the office. My daughter was also placed in the school and I decided not to bring my family as I anticipated that I could not go on like this for long and my transfer was imminent.

My neighbour was a very interesting person and quite senior to me by age but lower in rank. He immediately came to my house when he saw that my door was open and went on talking. He lived with his wife and she also worked in our company. Everybody wanted a company to pass the free time with and I was happy. His children were studying in Guwahati. When something special was made in their house, I got a share as a routine as I did not have any cook and made my food myself. Of course, most of the time, I was out of the station. One day, we were gossiping and one interesting topic came out. We had an office circular issued by HR that educational allowance would be applicable up to the second issue. I jokingly asked him since my second issue was twin whether both of them were eligible for the allowance as they both were my second issue. He said only one would be and I asked him why and if it is so, then which of my sons would be considered as my second issue. He had no answer but did not accept that there was a problem in the circular. He advised me to officially get a clarification. Since I had no productive work in my hand, I wrote to the HR for clarification on the matter as a timepass. Within a year, I was transferred to Guwahati under ED (project), which was headed by a very dynamic officer then. He was a very strict officer and once he was my SE at Shillong. Until leaving Shillong, my note on the educational allowance was going from table to table without any decision and almost after two years, they corrected the circular by issuing a fresh circular, this time correctly.

AT GUWAHATI

RESTORATION OF RANGANADI MACHINES

I took on rent one of my colleagues' flats, which was almost six km away from the office. During that time, I had a small Maruti 800 car that became too useful as travelling to-and-fro to the office on the city bus was very tiring. The department also allowed loans at a cheap rate of interest for vehicle procurement, so I took the advantage. The flat I had taken was on the first floor and had two flats on the same floor but the other one was empty. The house was quite big and had a big compound with separate parking. I got a lady who took care of my cooking, cleaning, and washing and I was relieved from such hazards. From day one, I was given a lot of work and I came back from the office always late. She had the key to my house and I kept some money with her so that whatever was required she could purchase. Though I never asked her where she spent the money, she always gave the expenditure details.

At that time, our Ranganadi project was commissioned and immediately on commissioning, all the three machines of 135 MW capacity had to be withdrawn due to a crack in the bottom bracket and heavy vibration.

ED (Project) had sent me and two of my colleagues, one from Kopili and another from Shillong, to solve the problem there. During our seven-hour journey to the project from Guwahati, we were discussing the probable reasons for the problem but could not come to a conclusion. From the OEM's side, Mr. Chakravorty came and we met after a long time. On the way, there was a famous Dhaba, where we stopped for our food. We took some beer and a meal and then again continued to the project through Banderdewa Assam Arunachal border gate, where inner line permits were required to enter Arunachal Pradesh. Our departmental officers kept those ready and were waiting for us at the gate. We reached the guest house and had some drinks when the project head came and briefed the problem along with the Engineer in charge of the powerhouse, Kamal, who was my ex-office roommate in Shillong. We were listening but nothing was going into our heads as we were almost drunk by then. We took an early breakfast and left for the powerhouse, which was quite far away and the road conditions were also very bad.

We inspected the machines one by one and found the crack almost at the same location of the bottom bracket for all the machines. After a detailed investigation, we ultimately found that the sole plate where the bracket stood was not properly grouted as required and the sole plates were disturbed. We accordingly directed to dismantle the first unit on an experimental basis and sole plates were re-erected and properly grouted in our presence. The bracket where that was cracked was gouged properly and welded round after round. After every round, radiography was carried out to see the perfection in welding. The machine was then re-erected and it behaved normally. The beam of the turbine inspection gallery was also found to be under-designed and additional support with a steel girder was provided. We started giving load gradually up to full load and there was no problem. The problem was resolved. Thereafter, the same modification was carried out in the other two machines also and all the machines were performing normally. We stayed there for nearly a month till the completion of all the three machines and came back. The project head and our ED project were very happy. As soon as I came back, the very next day he sent me to the Kameng project in Arunachal Pradesh, where there was some issue related to the construction of some roads along with two more officers. I asked him, "Boss, what can I do on a complete Civil construction matter?" but he forced me to go as he had a lot of faith in me. No more excuses, I moved the next morning and came back after a few days and submitted the report to him. That was a very elaborate report and the boss was happy.

During that period, another ED (Hydro) post was created and my earlier ED (Commercial) had taken charge. I was shifted under him. That time, our office was running from a rented house in Guwahati and we were facing a lot of seating problems. I had given a detailed proposal to my boss about the issue, prepared with the help of some of my colleagues, for submission to our new CEO, who was a very dynamic officer. Based on this proposal and some groundwork from our team, my company bought a prestigious building in Guwahati. Of course, by that time, I was transferred to Kameng HEP in Arunachal Pradesh in January 2004 on promotion as Deputy General Manager and Engineer in charge of Electro mechanical packages. When I got a posting in Guwahati again, later as ED, I did not get a proper place even to sit in the Guwahati office, which had been acquired by my company and the groundwork was done for the same by the very few of us. People forget what you contributed but remember what mistake you had made, however silly it may be. That is a reality; the opportunist always takes the advantage and such dirty things become a routine everywhere and the petty politics of those people become more visible in organisations with a weak administration. Those people who are behind the growth of the company do not have time for such petty things but the people who build their careers without any contributions always depend on their others' qualities to keep their bosses happy

Our new CEO during that time who acquired the Guwahati office was a very tough man and all were scared of him. No one dared to argue with him. In the Ministry also, he never met anyone below a level. One evening, I got a call from the PS of our CEO from Delhi. He told me that the CEO wanted to talk with me. I was scared as I did not know what mistake I had made.

The PS connected to the CEO.

"Mr Sarmah, can you go to Kameng now?"

He was straightway coming to business without any formalities.

Though it was quite late in the evening, I was scared to tell him no.

I said, "Yes, sir."

"Ok, you move," he said.

Then, he asked me, "If you start now, what time will you be there?"

I got an opportunity, so I told him it may take six to seven hours to reach Bhalukpung, the interstate border point where our temporary office was established.

Gathering a lot of courage as this was my first interaction with him, I asked him, "Sir will it be ok if I start early in the morning?"

"What time can you start?"

I said five o' clock.

He probed, "That means you will be there by 12 pm in that case?"

I said yes.

"Ok, you proceed in the morning."

I asked him, "Sir, what am I supposed to do there?"

"You are posted there," he told me bluntly.

I told him that I had not received any order.

He told me that before I reach Bhalukpong, my order would be there. Communication up to Bhalukpong was reasonably good.

I was dumbfounded. 15 days earlier, we had our promotion interview and I was expecting something. But I was not expecting that in such a hurry, he would order my departure from Guwahati. The ED came to my room hearing that the CEO was on a call with me. I told him what had happened.

IN THE KAMENG HYDROELECTRIC PROJECT

NEW PLACE, NEW RESPONSIBILITIES

I moved the next morning to Bhalukpong, not at five o' clock but around eight am and reached there around two pm, where I met my new boss KD, who was the General Manager and called as the HOP (head of the project), which was the new nomenclature that time. Bhalukpong, 56 km from Tezpur in Assam, is the entry point to Arunachal Pradesh's west Kameng district. The river Kameng, after completing all turbulent courses, enters Bhalukpong in a serene flow which provides a rare opportunity for adventure tourism and a beautiful picnic spot. Angling and river rafting are the principal tourist activities in Bhalukpong. Bhalukpong serves as a gateway to popular destinations like Tawang and Bomdila. The beautiful landscape with dense forests and the Himalayas make these places extremely beautiful. Bhalukpong is the entry point for the Tippi Orchid Research Centre, Chillipam Monastery, Lhagyala Gompa, and many more. Sangti Valley is the most serene place in West Kameng district.

The accommodation was scarce as very few houses were available for rent and our guest house was not ready. Luckily, Ashis, my old friend from Shillong, had taken a rented house as he was posted there a few months back and was staying with Ranjit. They allowed me as their third member of the mess. At least, I got a shelter.

By the time I reached, the HOP had received my transfer order with my Promotion as Engineer in Charge of All Electromechanical works. The CEO was telephoning him regarding my arrival. I reported to the CEO that I had reached and joined. He was laughing and told me that he was sure that I would perform well and conveyed his best wishes to me. I was so happy to talk to my CEO whom we only knew as a terror till then.

Kameng HEP was one of the huge projects of 600 MW capacity with 16 km of the tunnel with two km HRT with few 90-degree vertical shafts in HRT. Two dams. The main Bishom dam site was quite far off from the proposed powerhouse location by road. Ashis had recently joined as Senior Manager civil. There was no road available to the powerhouse site then. From Bhalukpong, with a lot of waterfalls on the way, the road went to Tawang, one of the most beautiful places covered by snow most of the time in an year. From Bhalukpong, after around 30 km, there was a diversion of the road going to Seppa, district HQ town and the main road went to Bomdila, Tawang. On the road to Seppa, there was a diversion point called Khuppi. From Khuppi, it is 30 km to the powerhouse location diverting from the Seppa road. The road to the powerhouse location was called KIMI and was under formation cutting stage and up to 14 km, it was "jeepable." Beyond that, as work was going on, we had to walk as the jeep could not go beyond that in those days. One day after my joining, I decided to go to the location to have a clear vision. Both Ashish and I started after lunch to the location and reached the 14 km point where we had a temporary Camp and stayed there. The next day early morning, Ashish and I started walking and reached there around 11' o'clock. Our one team of investigation Engineers were camping there. Three Engineers, Asanta, Anjan, and Amit were camping, totally isolated from the outside world and getting their food materials from the local nearby villages or someone who came from Bhalukpong. We also carried some for our young Engineers. They were staying in a *Chang Ghar* (House) made of bamboo and the great river Kameng was flowing 100 m away from the camp. What a beautiful sight! In Kameng, the discharge was very high and it was a snow-fed river, so the water was always available. The project was a run of the river scheme. On getting the news that we had reached there, the village headman who was quite young and educated came to meet us and told us that we had to have food with them and then only we could go. We were already hungry after 16 km of walking on that hilly road wherein every step we took had to be careful as loose stones were coming down the hill without notice. The headman had left and after half an hour, he came back with a big fish just caught by him from the river. He removed the scales of the fish and after washing, he made some surface cuts on the fish and removed the inside intestine, etc. and put ginger wrap with a little salt. He wanted to put chilli but I told him not to. Then, it was roasted in the fire lit for the purpose outside the house. Soon, it was ready. He brought some banana leaves and gave us the cut pieces. I have never tasted such a tasty fish preparation ever. By this time, our three musketeers prepared rice and dal and we had a great feast. Soon, we were in the proposed powerhouse location. I was appalled when I saw that the area near the powerhouse, which was the most suitable site and was already levelled by nature and was marked for making the permanent colony there instead of the 400 kV switchyard.

We came back in the evening and reached the 14 km camp and stayed again. More than 30 km walk that day makes us extremely exhausted. The caretaker arranged some local drinks for us which was very strong. I could not even take a single peg. We had our dinner and slept till late in the morning.

The next day, after reaching Bhalukpong, I told the HOP that the permanent colony should not be made at the location marked as that was the only and best location for the SY. He was not impressed and took the matter very casually. Without having any other way out, I had given it in writing not to use this land for any purpose other than switchyard. He told me that the SY could be anywhere but the permanent colony would be there. I told him that the colony can be anywhere but the switchyard should be nearest to the powerhouse and that was the only space available. I had given the information to the ED project as well as the Design office and based on my letter, the colony construction work was stopped by the ED project temporarily till a final decision was taken. I started studying the powerhouse drawings and found two major defects in the drawings. First, the tunnel system was made without a valve house and a 16 km Tunnel with a MIV pressure of 50 kg/cm2 would only depend on the surge shaft gate, which cannot be made hundred per cent sealed. The service bay was made on two different levels. One for unloading and one for assembly. Different EOT cranes were provided. I got very angry when I pointed out the defects to the person concerned and they took the matter as interference. I seemed to have hurt their ego. At that time, a panel of experts constituted by the CEO was visiting the project and I decided to place these three serious matters to them. My HOP was not interested to include these but upon my insistence, he agreed at the last minute and told me to handle these matters by myself with the expert panel as he felt those were an unnecessary waste of his time and therefore, I was not getting any support from him. The meeting of the expert panel was going on till midnight at hotel Luit at Tezpur and my agenda was placed at the last. I explained the details to them and told them that without a valve house, we will depend only on the surge shaft gate even for changing the seal of MIV and if there was a leak in the surge shaft gate which is always the case, we may be required to deplete the 16 km long tunnel and all the machine which are of 150 MW capacity would be out for long. After a lot of arguments, they agreed to my suggestion. My HOP realised the gravity of my points only after this meeting and he appreciated me for taking up these matters. Soon, the CEO approved the modification as suggested by me to have a valve house and one service bay, deleting the requirement of one extra EOT crane, and the location of the switchyard. After all this, my HOP took me into his confidence and the decisions were taken later regarding Electrical works always after discussing it with me. But as usual, there were always interdepartmental issues and conflicts, which were very common everywhere. He was a nice man always ready for help; I was no. 2 in the project till H.S Paul DGM joined the project and was senior to me, belonging to the civil cadre. He was such a nice person and everyone respected him as an elder brother; he had a very dirty tongue but a very clean heart.

There were few temporary hostels under construction at the powerhouse area for temporary accommodation of the officers and staff and the formation cutting of the road work was also going on at full speed by the Border Road Organisation.

One morning, I was awakened by some peculiar sound coming from the veranda outside of my house. I got up and told Ashis who was fully asleep. We both went out to find Ranjit who was a very lean and thin person exercising with a dumbbell and the sound was coming from his mouth only. It gave us a lot of entertainment and we enjoyed it so much.

Soon, I got a small house nearby the office but for me it was sufficient. I shifted to the new house. I prepared my food myself as there was no helping hand available. Ashish frequently came to my place and we took the food together. Earlier in Shillong, Pradip was taking care of the kitchen but here both of us were quite incompetent on the subject. I was waiting for the hostels to be ready so that we could shift to the hostels and the headache of preparing food could be avoided. My area of work was spread over three locations, first the powerhouse site, then at Khuppi where we will have a 132/33/11 kV substation, the Tenga dam site, a few kilometres away from Khuppi, and the main dam site at Bishom that was quite far away and took nearly six hours by road with pathetic road conditions from Khuppi. Khuppi area was always foggy all the time and people hardly saw the sun there. Frequent rain was another big hurdle in the works. We had given a deposit work to Powergrid for the construction of a 132 kV line from their Balipara SubStation(S/S) to Khuppi and Kimi, the powerhouse site with a 132/33 Kv S/s at Khuppi. Later, this 132 kV line would be used for evacuation along with two 400 kV outgoing lines from Kimi S/S. Our first job was making the distribution lines to all the work areas and the electrification of the colony.

The 132kV line was coming through extremely difficult terrain and in some locations, we had to change tower class to have a longer span. In a few locations, the tower locations were to be fixed at the hilltop and all construction materials like cement, sand, and aggregate. Steel material tower parts were to be carried on head load. One labour going with a bag of cement in the morning came back by evening and thus enough labour was required to be put. I was associated with various transmission lines earlier but the terrain here was the toughest we had encountered. I had to constantly visit these sites to expedite the process as the colonies were nearly getting completed and we started with DG sets for power supply that were stopped at midnight as power supply to work sites was critical. All worksites had also started and the power supply was through very costly Diesel sets. In the meantime, the road from Khuppi to Kimi was made motorable except for a few small bridges, where temporary arrangements by diversion of the road were made and in use till permanent braille bridges of small length that were under construction were completed. Gradually, we started to shift to the hostel. Similar hostels were also made at Khuppi and Bishom and in all these buildings, internal electrification work and power supply were to be made. We were taking up parallelly the 11kv lines to work sites where the contractors were putting their 11/0.4 Kv transformers. So that by the time the 132 KV lines were ready, we were also ready with our internal distribution system. We had internally arranged DG sets and the cables were laid to all the hostels for power supply from evening to midnight and in the mornings, a few hours till the 132kV line was ready. We used to stop the power supply at midnight to save diesel as bringing diesel from Bhalukpong was difficult and had to bring in gallons as no tanker was coming to Kimi and we did not have the storage facility then. The engineers would shout *Murdabad murdabad* (Shame, Shame!) as soon as the power was cut off as if it was my fault for being in charge of the power supply. Later on, it became a routine and I went to bed only after the slogan shouting was stopped. We all enjoyed this thoroughly. People find various means to enjoy their life under the most difficult living conditions. Carrying every material from Bhalukpong was difficult and as there was no communication under such circumstances, the unity amongst the various teams automatically increased and the people were ready to help each other. However, people in comfortable areas find this thing missing and they naturally become self-centred and do not want to leave their comfort posting to a project posting.

We faced very serious challenges in awarding the petty contracts as there were so many contractors bidding without any required paper and creating chaos in the project regularly if they did not get the contract. Those who were successful came with the bill within a week for full payment without even starting the work. I worked in so many places but here, the situations were extremely bad and I was scared for the safety of my Engineers as the law enforcement had no meaning there then. By facing a lot of difficulties on a daily basis, we did our internal colony electrification job only by God's grace and the unending tolerance level of my engineers.

We got the 5 MVA 132/11k V transformer on-site and kept it ready for charging and was waiting for the line to be completed and energised.

I was normally getting free by the evening and all officers were doing all kinds of jobs after coming back from the site or office. Office buildings were also temporarily made till the main complex was built. Some played cards, some billiards, some drinks and gossip, and some tried their hand at cooking with our cooks. A different life altogether. However, there was a charm in this life also and all found their way to enjoy their own way after being back from our work sites. There was no issue of hierarchy and all lived like a family. Going home also became very difficult due to transportation issues and roads where formation cutting was going on made transportation difficult due to frequent landslides. There was an insect called "dumdim," which was like a small mosquito, a great menace and people with black dresses were more prone to their attack. They bite in finger joints, ears, and neck or any soft part, which creates havoc, especially when we wear black. People used white hand gloves to protect themselves.

We had completed the 132 kV line and the Sub Station was ready and we extended the power supply to all the work locations and internal colony. All were getting 24 hours of power supply. I was constantly in touch with BSNL, the only provider of telephone communication. I met the General Manager at Itanagar, the capital of Arunachal, where he was posted and once I took him to our site to make him understand our difficulty. At that time, their Director from Delhi was supposed to visit Itanagar and I went to meet him there but he straight away went to Dimapur, The North Eastern hub of BSNL. With one of my officers, I went to Dimapur at night itself and met him there to explain our difficulties. Mr. Dutta, GM Itanagar, also requested on our behalf. The Director instructed to divert one exchange which was available with them for some places. Soon, we had the telephone exchange working from KIMI. It was possible only due to the help offered by the GM Itanagar, Mr. Dutta and our constant follow-ups. It was in 2005 last.

The communication revolution within the last decade has made us dependent on mobile phones and we cannot survive nowadays without a smartphone and high-speed internet. We had already commissioned our intercom exchanges at all three locations. I put Ranjit to look after the works at Khuppi and Phukan was put at Bishom. I used to visit Bishom once a month.

In the Senior executive hostel, a Billiard board was placed as our HOP was very fond of Billiard. People like me who do not know anything about Billiard soon learned it and played it sometimes when free. A volleyball court was also made and people used to play volleyball till late at night and the shouting went on till midnight. With the improvement of our communication, our problems with the local contractors increased manifold and almost every day we had some problem or the other.

One helipad was also made ready within the project area for the VIPs visit. After completion of the helipad, a big picnic was arranged there, where all nearby villagers were participating along with all our officers. There were so many beautiful women and girls participating. The society was very open and all of them were mixing up with all of us like their family members. *Apong*, a local drink, was served to all in bamboo glasses (*Chunga*). If you were not taking the offers, they would feel insulted and I took one but the environment was such that we had to go on continuously. People were dancing with music at full blast. I saw a very beautiful young woman in a white dress who was dancing very beautifully and looked very pretty and being a bit drunk, I could not remove my eyes from her. The village head man noticed that and he held my hand and dragged me to that woman for dancing. We danced quite for some time and gradually everyone started dancing. But we become the centre of attraction. She was very beautiful and danced so well.

After a few days, Saraswati puja was celebrated at the project and HOP, a very jolly and culturally active person, decided to bring special performers from Guwahati. Before the guest artist started, our project talents were performing. One of the surprises was a dance by a girl Chinsaw from my office staff. She was very shy but given such a brilliant piece of dance, she became famous overnight and in all future programmes, her name was included automatically.

In the meantime, a separate HOP was posted for Bishom Dam as communication from Kimi to Bishop was very tiresome and the work could not be monitored properly. With his appointment, I was relieved of the responsibility for the power supply at the Bishom and it was taken over by another officer posted there. I got a big relief as travelling to Bishom was a big headache due to the road conditions.

The powerhouse excavation works were going on and I pressurised the civil counterpart to release the service bay area excavated fast and handed over to me to lay the Earth mat. After a month or so, that was handed over to us and we completed the earth mat for the service bay.

At that time, we hired a new building at Bhalukpong, which was used as our guest house. Our monthly review meeting was held there so that the engineers were getting a break, even though the review meeting was a very serious affair. That day, the meeting was going on and I and MS, who was in charge of the Tenga dam, were sitting nearby. At lunch break, I finished my food early and went to the roof to have a cigarette comfortably. At that time, only MS and I were the addicted smokers; the others mostly had one or two a day. MS was searching for me and asked the caretaker about me and he told MS, "Sir had gone up." MS thought something else and he shouted, "We were together half an hour back how he has gone up so quickly." The caretaker had to explain to him again—at that time the HOP was also there—that I had gone to the rooftop to smoke cigarettes and had not gone up finally. There was great fun on these issues and the HOP in every meeting told me "Sarmah, do not go up otherwise MS will again shout." Those were the small things giving us entertainment and we never missed such opportunities or forgot about them. It gives us immense pleasure when we look back on our leisure time.

Soon, I was called for an interview and within a few days, my promotion order as General Manager was out but I was transferred to the project where I started learning about the project execution and that was the Kopili Hydro Electric project. Immediately after the order, the CEO told me that I should make a move to Kopili urgently by the next morning as there was an accident in the Khandong Surge shaft gate where one of our employees was dead. The CEO seemed to be very offended by the incumbent HOP and forced me to move fast. But all the site officers were not releasing me without a formal farewell followed by a dinner, where till morning all were enjoying food, drinks, music, and dance. Even all the ladies joined the dinner and enjoyed it till morning. I was so grateful to all the officers and staff for the love and respect they showered on me. Early in the morning when I was about to leave for Guwahati on the way to Kopili, one of my lady staff came to me and gave me a Sweater she had made by hand for me. I was so grateful. I left the project after saying bye to all my colleagues. I was happy that within the three years I was there, I did the major design changes and made all the infrastructure for going ahead with the job, including the communication.

As a habit, I always tell myself: never expect any good words from anybody because people will forget what you have done shortly and a new batch of people will come and take over, who will have no idea or interest to know what good we have done and under what difficult situations but they find out at least one defect that someone previous to them had made. Decisions are taken at a time with certain limitations out of the alternatives available by selecting the best as per one's view or those that are logically correct. No one will understand the situations in which such decisions were required to be taken at that time when situations are totally changed at present. When the 4G service is available who will use the WT; when the internet is available what telex will do? Those automatically vanished and now the new generation of Engineers cannot even believe that there was stencil paper and tender documents were made like that. Decisions are always time- and situation-specific and cannot be reviewed by comparing the facilities available much later when there is fast-developing technology or change in situations. The action taken by the earlier generation opened the road for newer inventions and the different working methodologies have been adopted as the years passed.

I always tell myself that if I have to tell lies to my own conscience, then I am not correct. I strictly followed this throughout my career. Whatever I do, I should be satisfied with my inner self, what others say later is immaterial to me. Maybe, I was correct to a certain extent as I have observed such reactions from people during my service period itself.

KOPILI HEP WELCOMES
AGAIN

TO KOPILI AS HEAD OF THE PROJECT

I reached Guwahati. On the way, while I was travelling to Guwahati, the CEO called me over the phone several times to check whether I was moving to Kopili or not; at that time Guwahati and some areas on the National Highway and some towns were getting connected by mobile phone, and I had my first Nokia phone from Tezpur with connection from the only service provider BSNL.

I talked to HOP Kopili who was a close friend of mine and a few years senior to me and he was in Guwahati. He told me that he was going to the project next morning. We decided to go together and my vehicle was following us as I carried all my essentials in the vehicle. The next morning, after a long time since I moved to Kopili HEP, I started learning my initial lessons about project executions.

The HOP briefed me about what was happening at the project while we were on the road to Kopili and we discussed how we had solved the problem at Ranganadi during its commissioning time. I came to know a lot from him regarding the actual situation in the project. He dropped me at the guest house for lunch. I was so thrilled to see the full reservoir and the ambience of the guest house, which was one of the locations I enjoyed the most. I rang up the CEO, informing him that I reached the project and he instructed me to take over charge immediately. But my friend was not in a hurry to give me the charge and he wanted some pending works to be finished before he left the project. He handed over the charge after a week and this delay helped me to understand the project issues, which he briefed me in detail. My friend Tilak was also there to assist me in the civil wing as Head of the civil wing and Hari, my friend from operation and maintenance, was also reporting to me. Finance head was a senior man and he lost in rank as he left the corporation in between and came back in the same rank a few years later. During this period, his juniors had gotten promoted. He was a straight-talking person and I respected him for his age and experience even though then he was reporting to me.

On the day of my taking charge, a grand farewell was organised to the outgoing HOP. He was there from his joining more than twenty years and he was a very unhappy man. I also felt bad. The next day morning, he left the project. I was at his house to say goodbye. The building department started painting and repairing the house promptly and I shifted to my official quarter without delay. I also got a boy who was staying with me to prepare my food.

I was briefed that a major problem had been observed in the project, both in Khandong and Kopili, where all the underwater parts were getting damaged and all water-carrying pipes including transformer cooler pipes were facing regular failure. A very abnormal phenomena that we could not properly identify at the beginning but we doubted it had to do with the reservoir water becoming acidic. The same was tested and found to be correct as the Ph value was below four. Further, an order was placed with the Geological Survey of India for investigating the matter. The area beyond the reservoir was full of coal but with high Sulphur content. The coal was excavated on open cast mining and gradually became exposed to the rainwater and the water reached the reservoir as sulphuric acid. The matter was reported to HQ and a detailed presentation was done in the HOP's meeting at Shillong taken by the CEO. A team of all the expert agencies of the government was formed to further study the matter. This was a phenomenon nowhere reported in India earlier and all are actually confused about what to suggest. We were running the power station with great risk of transformer or bearing failure, which was becoming common and we were taking all trial-and-error methods for rectifications. We were specifically worried about the bearings and the transformer coolers, where the cooler pipes leaked and mixed up with oil.

After lunch, I went to Kopili powerhouse, where two more units were commissioned after I had left Shillong to Doyang and for which all electrical mechanical contracts were awarded during my time in Shillong. Tilak and Hari and junior officers were going along with me. The Annual maintenance work was going on in Unit 2 and rotor lowering was planned for the next day. That was a Thursday and someone was telling me to defer it by a day. However, I did not believe in such things and told my engineers to go ahead. Most of the project Engineers worked with me earlier somewhere or the other and knew very well that I would not tolerate works remaining pending and I went to the roots of the problem to understand the problem thoroughly. They were careful with me as I never spared anyone who told lies or covered up facts. I used to tell them, "As human beings, we all are prone to mistakes which are natural but do not try to cover it up when you come to know the mistake." They were all competent and experienced engineers and needed only a pat on the back to be motivated. I had a very competent team there. Next, we visited the Khandong plant. When I was in Kameng, one additional unit was put near the Khandong powerhouse, which was an unmanned powerhouse and was controlled by the Khandong powerhouse. The Khandong surge shaft had two gates, one for Khandong 1 and 2 and one for the Extension unit. The accident happened in the surge shaft gate there and it was the most priority job to restore the gates as it was the monsoon time and the reservoir was full. A contract was awarded from HQ for this job and I was from morning to evening busy with my Engineers and the engineer and workman of the contractor. With a lot of planning and effort, the gate was lifted without the Surge shaft EOT crane, which had gotten damaged during the time of the accident when the operator was killed.

Shortly after the replacement of the seal and the repair of the EOT crane of the Surge shaft gate, the gate was lowered and tested successfully. During the entire period, the CEO was behind me until its successful completion. He was very happy and issued an appreciation letter to me and all my engineers. Kopili Unit 2 was also back to grid and all the units of the project were running with a hundred per cent capacity 24×7. We were relaxed and the project engineers were very busy maintaining the machines so that there was no forced shut down under the acute situation created by the acidic water.

I started sitting in the office and started discussing project matters with all the officers one by one to know any issues and of the action being taken. I was shocked to see the file noting of O&M head and Head of Finance and while reading, I just imagined a scene where the both were standing before me putting their sword out and on war. I called both of them to my room to have a cup of tea. I told my PS not to allow anyone inside. I had a frank talk with both of them and told them in very clear terms that I did not want this type of file noting in future and hence closed those files without approval. I told them that in future, such files should not come to me and if there were any difference of opinion between them, they should sort that out through discussion and might also discuss with me before fighting over files. Both agreed. I told them that I only monitor the deadline and will not interfere in their job till I found everything was going well and on time. The message was loud and clear for all officials in the project and so no such incident happened later.

My previous HOP was planning one botanical garden in the project and he was having some discussions with the botanical survey of India. I liked the idea very much and soon it became a pet project for me. My next-door neighbour at Shillong was the senior officer attached by the Botanical Survey of India for this job. I put R&B division, especially Mr. Sonowal Manager (Civil), for this job and they were so thrilled to work on this project. The RETs (Rare, Endangered & Threatened) species of plants in the entire district were identified and various orchids were planted in the area earmarked for the project surrounding a water body fully cleaned. There was a lot of scrap steel material lying in the store. My Senior Manager (C) had designed a walking bridge connecting both sides of the water body and was using a welder on daily charge basis and the bridge was done departmentally. It was looking so beautiful and became a centre of attraction. In my career, I was involved with a lot of works with machines but this is the work that had given me the utmost satisfaction. I visited this place very frequently and became very relaxed. We had a school with classes up to 12th run by Vivekananda Kendra, sponsored by my company, where I visited to meet the children rather than the teachers frequently. I enjoyed being with them and sometimes I also took one or two classes. The teachers were also very friendly with me and they were happy that after a long time, the HOP was taking interest in the school matters.

TERROR STRIKE

The initial days of my life in the project were going on smoothly but shortly problems started. One afternoon, when I was back from lunch to the office, I got a call from an unknown person demanding a huge sum of money and told me that he belonged to an underground outfit. I did not pay much interest. But later I came to know that those were the terror group that was creating much disturbances in the district. The man went on calling me and threatening me almost regularly. I reported the matter to the District Superintendent of police and Deputy Commissioner, in addition to the local police station. One day, he sent a letter over fax, making the demand in his organisational pad and gave a deadline for the payment. I immediately informed this to the district authority and our HQ, in turn, took the matter up with all the authorities. I was assured that whatever was required to safeguard us would be provided and I should not worry. Security in the project was tightened and some additional force was deployed. But providing security was very difficult as the Kopili power station was 24 km away from the Colony and Khandong was also around 10 km. On both sides of the roads were jungles and these terrorists could be anywhere. Whenever I came to the office, I got phone calls from these people indicating that somebody was monitoring my movements. During the Bihu festival in January 2008, I came home for a few days and Tilak was in charge. But in the evening, I came to know that these group had attacked our Kopili power station and fired randomly, killing some of our staff and security people and one local person. The CEO called me that night and I started for the project that night itself as all the employees were totally demoralised. By the time I reached there, it was around four pm. All the employees and their families were in my house. The powerhouse was stopped. The body had been taken to district HQ for post mortem. After a lot of persuasion, I could convince the employees and their families and I went to the powerhouse even after a lot of objections from the security agencies, which were camped inside the project to assist the State police. My friend and colleague Gogoi was always with me guiding, helping, and coordinating with the employees and he was an old hand in Kopili who was respected by all.

The powerhouse operations were restored the next day and the shift duty people were transported with full escort. Two mini trucks that were recently purchased for some other projects had been diverted to our project and sent to Guwahati for converting them bullet proof immediately. The situation in the project suddenly became very grim. None were coming out of their house and all social activities totally came to a standstill. I was getting regular calls from those people demanding the money and they were saying that what had happened was just a trailer and if we did not pay, we would face more such incidence. I reported these things to the District and State authorities on a daily basis and I was on regular touch with all law enforcing authorities. After 10-15 days, the CEO and the Director (Personnel) visited the project for a few hours and returned without meeting the employees, which created a lot of resentment. I had to accompany them to Shillong and the next day to New Delhi. I was in the top bureaucrats' room briefing the status of the project at that time when I got a call from my colleague Gogoi from Kopili. He informed me that those people had striked again on the convoy carrying our employees on shift, killing seven people. I put my speaker phone on and I asked the officer to speak either in English or Hindi so that everyone in the room could listen to what was happening. He arranged a meeting with the concerned top officials and I briefed them also. I came back the next day by the first flight and reached the project. The situation was extremely bad. I was gheraoed by all the women of the project crying and all sat down and

I with folded hands requested them to go back home but nobody was going back and urging me to solve the issue. I was also sitting with them and asking them what action from me could convince them. There was no reply. I was concentrating on how to come out of these grave situations. The powerhouse was closed. The power supply line to the powerhouse was damaged as security forces made a lot of return fire, even though none of the terrorists was killed or injured but the line had snapped and required to be restored to run the emergency system of the powerhouse immediately for the safety of the machines. I decided to go to the powerhouse as four of my Engineers were trapped there and they had to be evacuated. They stayed back there as the emergency system of the powerhouse needed to be run. Unless certain systems were kept operational, there would be big problems with restarting the machines and the safety of the power station. The security forces who were present there to help the local police first did not allow me to go but I persisted and with full security, I went to the powerhouse with the Utility team to restore the transmission line. Nearly 20 soldiers were guarding them during the restoration process, which was completed by midnight. Gogoi organised a few volunteers to go to the powerhouse to replace the trapped Engineers and we carried sufficient food materials and other essentials while going there. Tilak and Hari were controlling the situation at the colony, which was very tense as the employees' families were very frightened. By late night, I came back with the trapped Engineers and the Utility Engineers, leaving the volunteered Engineers with some additional guards at the powerhouse. The cook of the canteen remained there with our Engineers. I was so grateful to them, who had volunteered, risking their own lives for the power station. The power supply to the station was also restored at night itself.

A similar incident happened in the Cement plant, a few kilometres away from our project and a few officers were also killed there.

I had repeated meetings with all the unions and Engineers to bring the project back to normalcy. I was not prepared to bow down to these cowards at any cost. In the meantime, DGP, Assam, and Senior Police officers came and visited us. For a short term, one additional team of paramilitary forces was placed for the security and an arrangement was made to transport the employees in bulletproof vehicles. The two mini trucks which were recently diverted to our project were converted to bulletproof vehicles and the shift officials were taken by those vehicles only with full escort at their front and back. There were two roads to reach the powerhouse. Normally, earlier only the shortage route via the surge shaft was used. Now, we planned to use both the roads and information was given to the drivers at the last minute about which route to take. The security forces were giving escort to the team. Instead of regular shifts and to reduce movement, we temporarily decided to send two batches of shift people together. But even after all these arrangements, people were not ready to go which was very natural as their families were not allowing them to move. After a lot of persuasion and pleading over the first few days and by telling them that I would also move with the convoy, the people gradually accepted and after four days of shut down, the machine started coming one by one. I made arrangements for keeping the families informed on a daily basis and met them frequently to reassure them. After these two incidents, the security was made very elaborate but I was still got threats every now and then over the phone and sometimes through satellite phones also and some letters were dropped for me at any location. All phone numbers were provided to the security agencies. As all the employees on shift were facing great trouble to be there for 72 hours without proper arrangement for their rest and sleep, the bedding materials were sent to them and while one shift was taking rest, the other was taking care of running the units. I had decided to make a two-storied building at the powerhouse complex as we did not know how long the problem would persist and my Engineers were not getting a proper place to rest after taking all the responsibility voluntarily. The building was made very quickly as the people were working day and night and stayed there only.

In the meantime, I had taken a series of special welfare measures in the locality starting from constructing a ladies' common room at the local college and providing a sufficient quantity of books for their library as well as building toilets and boundary walls in a few schools, a market complex, interior roads in the market, and a water supply arrangement in various nearby villages to help the local population who were really poor. These were carried out much before the government introduced the CSR (corporate social responsibility) programme for the PSUs. I got overwhelming support from the people, especially the youth of those places. We had also taken care of Haflong Industrial Training institute so that skilled manpower could be produced and given the opportunity to stand on their own feet.

I discussed all local area development programmes with Barman Sir, a senior citizen of the area and an ex-principal of a local school. He was a respected figure in that area and all local people listened to him. I observed that the people from the area remained totally isolated from the other areas of the state and mostly remained inside their locality and hence were not aware of the development that was happening outside. I invited all the school principals of that area to my chamber for a cup of tea and proposed to send a batch of students from their schools to Kolkata, along with some of my officers, and I would sponsor the entire programme. To my utter surprise, I did not get a single name from any of the principals. I called Barman Sir to my office chamber and told him about this. He was laughing. When asked why he was laughing.

"Sarmah, you made a major mistake," he said.

I was curious to know what mistake I had made.

He told me that I have gone too far to Kolkata. If it was Shillong or Guwahati, I would have gotten some names. I understood and later realised that.

Football was very popular in the villages and was a great unifier. Considering the same, I started the first club football tournament, sponsored by my company where all local village teams participated and it was a grand success. People there were football lovers and practically crazy about football. The participation exceeded our expectations. I still feel that sports is one of the biggest unifiers and the younger generation can be kept away from those divisive forces if sports are taken on a bigger scale. First club football tournament has proved that beyond doubt.

While going to Khandong power station, we always observed that some water was coming to the Khandong powerhouse continuously near the entrance to the powerhouse through seepage, and it was increasing day by day. We could not understand at first where from the water was coming and after a lot of investigation, we confirmed that this must be leakage from the tunnel. I requested HQ for allowing the shut-off of the three Khandong units for inspection of the tunnel when water level of the reservoir was low to avoid generation losses. After a lot of deliberation and hesitation, HQ finally allowed us to go ahead and we had taken the units shut down and the tunnel was depleted. The valve house and surge shaft gate were closed and inspection started. We found two major holes in the tunnel, which required to be grouted at high pressure consuming a very high quantity of cement. After the grouting, we gradually filled up the tunnel and units were back to Grid. We had also taken this period for annual maintenance of all the three units also by preponing the same so that total yearly downtime remained almost the same. There was no leakage observed at the Khandong site after that. It was a very risky and sophisticated job and Engineers were therefore avoiding dewatering of tunnel earlier but my team led by Tilak and Raj made it possible and we were very satisfied with the outcome.

KOPILI REST HOUSE INAUGURATION

After the Kopili rest house was made ready and furnished with canteen and food storage facilities, I asked our CEO if he could make a visit to Kopili to inaugurate the building. He had given me a date. The day before the scheduled date, I asked for his programme over the phone. He told me that due to some important meeting, he would not be able to come and asked me to request the Director Technical instead but he also first agreed and later refused to come because of some urgency. We made the inauguration plaque every time but there was no use for it. No senior official was willing to come to Kopili project, which created serious problems at the site. Those plaques must still be lying in the scrap store. I requested the Deputy Commissioner who was a personal friend of mine to do the inauguration. The next day, he sent a messenger with a letter, saying that the surrender of those terrorists was in process within a short time and as those people will surrender, he was not in a position to come out from the District HQ, which he regretted. The three of us—Tilak, Hari, and I—discussed the matter. We decided that when our employees were facing all kinds of problems and were sleeping behind the control panels when their accommodation was ready, we should not wait for these formalities and we ourselves would inaugurate the accommodation. In Khandong, we made eight Assamese-type of buildings with canteen so that people could stay without any difficulty and a high boundary wall was made surrounding these buildings with armed forces placed at the gate.

We did not invite anyone except the employees of Khandong and I inaugurated those camps. There was no problem then.

The Deputy Commissioner who was the head of the district administration made frequent visits to the project earlier and he never stayed in our guest house. He always came at odd hours to my house with a few cooks and helpers relaxing in my living room with a dim power light on. He listened only to the music of *Bhupen Hazarika* and went on having drinks for a few hours. He also left suddenly at odd hours. I understood he did so only for his security as all were affected badly during that period from those people and the administration was also not excluded.

The day we planned to inaugurate the Kopili building, all three of us Tilak, Hari, and I were in a school where we made toilets for the students. The principal invited us and requested several times to dedicate those constructions to the school students. The inauguration was done and from there I came to the office to see if any urgent work was there and then we moved to Kopili powerhouse. We did not invite anybody as this was just a formality and we were forced to do it as none of the big shots had agreed to come. We did it and Tilak and Hari came back after the ceremony and I stayed back so that I could personally supervise certain major maintenance work going on at that time and also to see the quality of the food being served to my Engineers and staff there. I was with them till around three pm and came back to my house. Two officers, one from CRPF and another from BSF, were waiting for me at my residence. They told me that a security review meeting would be held that evening at the Security camp where all the commanding officers of the forces present in that area and their bosses would be there and they told me that my presence also was required. I told them that within half an hour, I would be there and they left.

I took a bath and Deep, my cook, gave me a cup of tea and I left for the meeting. It continued till past nine pm and dinner was also served. Naturally, the drinks were also served in army style. This was a very fruitful meeting and all were giving their inputs and took a common strategy as those people were likely to lay down their arms and surrender within the next 10 days. They were worried with the information that certain people might not surrender on that day and might create some more trouble and accordingly, they made some planning and what we were required to do was informed to me. After dinner, I came back home and got a shock seeing that all my officers were in my house. All bad dreams were coming to my head that something might have happened again. I jumped out of my car and asked Tilak what was the matter but no one responded. I was more and more worried. I scolded Tilak to tell me what had happened. Then he opened up:

"Don't you know, you have a transfer order."

I got my transfer order one week back and Pradip was supposed to take my charge.

I told him that yes, I knew and talked about my discussion with Pradip who told me that he would be on leave for a few days and had requested me to stay a few days so that he got a brief from me about the Kopili situation, both technically and situation wise, as the project had issues quite sensitive. I agreed that after he came and after briefing to him only, I will move to Shillong, my new place of posting.

One of my colleagues who was GM and HOP in our Tripura project had gotten promoted as my boss two days back. He had also informed me that he would come within the next few days to understand the situation. And I should not leave the project till then. I had agreed.

Tilak knew about this as I had told him earlier.

As the surrender ceremony was scheduled in the same week, the situation in the project became normal and people started to move openly then. But who knows if someone was still left out from surrendering and created any problem; so, I advised all to be careful and movement to be strictly restricted.

I talked to Tilak regarding my discussion with Pradip and my new boss.

Then he said, "No, that is not the matter."

A fresh order was out giving the cause that one of the machines in Doyang had a generator failure and my services were required there urgently. I was stand released from Kopili, cancelling my earlier order of transfer to Shillong. This order was also issued in a hurry and not from the personnel department and was signed by my new boss only, who had asked me two days back not to leave till his visit and the generator failure happened 10 days back. Not getting me on line or being intentionally scared to contact me directly, he told my officers to convey to me to contact him as soon as I was back. I understood what was happening. This man had no guts to talk to the concerned officer on any issues and depended on their informers who are from the lowest level and representing some union or association for information. Those people did not understand the problem itself, forget about the solutions. One of such groups had created a problem in running the project and gheraoed me one day in the office for quite a long time and I did not care and went on doing my work in my office chamber till late hours. And they had to get back. One of their leaders had made certain serious irregularities and I threatened to hand him over to the police as I cannot withstand any kind of indiscipline. They were waiting for an opportunity to throw me out of the project and when these two men were in the chair of Power, they acted. They were not invited to the rest house inauguration at Kopili; therefore, they were immediately behind me giving a lot of misinformation resulting in this order. The man who talked to me two days back to remain in Kopili till he visited had signed that order for me to stand released and he wanted me to talk to him.

I told my officers to go back home but none went, they wanted to protest. I said nothing, I was leaving that night itself handing charge to Tilak who was the next senior man there. My Engineers arranged my farewell then and there only with whatever stock of drinks were with them and prepared some snacks. We finished it all. Deep was telling me dinner was ready but after all this, my tummy was full and did not take anything. Then I rang my so-called boss, maybe it was around 11 pm. He had become my boss two days ahead and he was also a HOP two days before and had created a scene at HQ when he was transferred to Kopili when the trouble was going on to get a retention order. I told him thank you for the order and for helping me get out of the project early. He must have been waiting to hear me plead for my retention but unfortunately got an appreciation from me for the transfer. I told him that since it is a stand release order, I was not spending the night also in the project and would leave the project at 11:45 pm. There was an urgent meeting fixed at Haflong, the District HQ by the Deputy commissioner, which I was supposed to attend the next day. But I cancelled my programme to Halflong and moved to Golaghat at midnight after handing over the charge to Tilak, who sent my belongings later. The officers were demoralised but for such personal matters, I never requested anybody for favour and that is why I was not deputed for a foreign training in my 36 years of dedicated career.

The security forces and commanders with whom I was there a few hours earlier were very surprised and bid me farewell by shaking hands and I left for Golaghat and reached there early in the morning.

My action had put my authorities in a serious dilemma as they were anticipating that I would request for a stay which I did not make.

MOVING TO DOYANG AS THE HOP

REPAIR OF GENERATOR

The same evening, I left for Doyang HEP, the powerhouse where I kept my footprints, again welcoming me. No one at HQ was expecting me to join there so fast as we could avail 12 days of leave on interstate transfers. I took charge from the DGM who was at that time holding charge temporarily.

I called a meeting of all the officers to know the status of the work of the unit whose generator was damaged. I found that there was a meeting with the OEM for the completion of repair work within seven months at a huge cost. I got very angry and told my engineers that I was not going as per the minutes and the machine had to be back by 45 days and would be done departmentally. I asked my Engineers where the problem area was and they told me some materials were urgently required and some skilled technicians were also required as those people were not available or posted at the project. Within the last 10 years, there were a lot of changes and the telephone was now a reality there. Some VSAT arrangements were also made and the internet also was available but at a very slow speed.

I called the Unit in charge of OEM in Mumbai where the required materials were made. Fortunately, the Unit in charge was my old friend and I told him that I joined the project and I needed his help in getting some material which list I mailed to him and he had to dispatch the material without waiting for the formal order. He told me that he would check the availability within an hour. Soon, he rang me back to inform that the materials were available and he already ordered for packing and dispatching without waiting for the order. He told me that he had full faith in me and knew my working style. As the items were not heavy, I told him to send them by air courier and to send me his quotation. I told the head of finance and head of O&M to sit in my chamber and process the offer received from him and the order should be placed by the next day. They worked till late hours and the orders were placed. Within the next three days, the material reached Guwahati where I placed my truck already to collect the material and came back. In the meantime, I was talking to the contractor who erected the Doyang Units and I knew every one of their skilled people by name. I talked to their boss and gave the names of the people I required at my site. He said that that group was then working in Bhutan on some hydro project. I requested him to divert them for a month and those people also reached the site within seven days. I ensured that there should not be any delay in the decision, so the HOF and the Head of O&M were told to sit in my chamber to process all matters in discussion with one another so that there was no file tossing from one to another. The people of Doyang knew me very well and loved and treated me as one of their family and cooperated fully. The next requirement was two winders, which was a very specialised job and the only source was OEM. With my contacts, I managed to get them and an order was placed for that skilled manpower from OEM. With all arrangements made, I was relaxed and went to my home for a few days after giving proper instruction to my team who were very happy and my trust in their capabilities raised their morale and motivated them. Earlier it seemed that they had a serious decision-making crisis as the earlier HOP and the next in charge had never worked in the machines. Work was going on fine and I was quite happy with the progress after I came back from home for a few days but I was taking the report of progress daily. My boss tried to contact me several times but I avoided it. For information, he was dependent on my lower-level employees who did not know what was going on as they had no idea about the machine and my younger engineers were too frustrated with him. He was unable to give a proper reply to the CEO regarding the progress even though we had sent progress reports as routine to him without any elaboration. My Engineers at the project got a breathing space when I took over. I stayed in the plant till late for their morale-boosting and made the HR take care of those people working late with food, etc. On the 38th day, the Unit was ready and stood the high voltage test. But a peculiar thing happened after a successful HV test as when we tried to synchronise the Unit to Grid, it immediately tripped showing Stator Earth's fault again. All were so disappointed. All the hard work went in vain it seemed. I called everyone to the control room and all had a cup of tea to cool our minds. I then told one of my engineers to disconnect the stator leads from the bus duct and to megger the stator. The megger value was perfect. I was so happy as there was no problem with the repaired stator and the fault was somewhere else. I told all my team to go back home and take some rest and come to the powerhouse at seven pm. All the boys after these sudden happenings were demoralised and confused, so I left them for some time to get refreshed.

I was sitting on the machine floor taking a cigarette; unfortunately, I did not have anyone to consult as well. There were the shift Engineers as the other two units were running. I decided on my action plan and left for the guest house as I did not occupy my quarter and stayed in the guest house. At seven pm, all of us met and I told them how to go about it from the next day. We went on checking the segment-wise up to the transformer and ultimately the fault was located at a PT in the LAVT cubicle, which was the least anticipated point. The unit came back exactly on the 42nd day. My boss, during the process, constantly tried to disturb me with all kinds of nasty communications, warning letters, advisories, etc., which I simply put in the dustbin as I knew he could not harm me any further as whatever he could do, he had already done. With the successful restoration of the unit, all who were behind me were compelled to write appreciation letters to me which I had given to my team who were those persons who deserved all the credit. The seven months' schedule was completed by my departmental Engineers within the 42nd day. That was a great achievement for our team. But it created problems for me as my relationship with my immediate boss worsened further. What he briefed the CEO about me was all found to be wrong.

CHUBBY NALA BRIDGE

Another major work front was opened. One of the   important and large villages was practically cut off from the project area as soon as the reservoir was filled and the villagers had to come to the project through a very long route. They demanded after the commissioning of the project for a bridge over the reservoir connecting the village and they did not allow to raise the water level to its full capacity. They went to the HQ. After a lot of deliberation, it was agreed that the construction of one of the longest 600 ft braille bridges over the reservoir linking both sides would be done. Work was started 9-10 years back but for whatever might be the reason, the work was stopped then. There was no progress on this front. After I joined, I was directed to take up the job and my team made a plan for restarting the work. Our earlier experience in the project helped us a lot. With a lot of obstructions from various quarters, the work was progressing well and the Deputy Commissioner who was a very nice man came very frequently to the bridge construction site and monitored the progress. The state government at the Chief Ministers' level was also interested to have this bridge and various cabinet ministers also paid regular visits. Our team was doing excellent work though there were a lot of problems coming from various quarters.

Days were passing smoothly as all the machines were running fine. I concentrated on the development of the colonies as still some people were staying in the temporary colony made during construction time and those were in very bad conditions. I had given a presentation in the HOP meeting taken by the CEO at Shillong in this regard and it was in principle agreed in those meetings to take up the renovation or new construction work. I had taken it to the CEO when he visited the project and showed him the conditions of the quarters and how the employees were living and he agreed that the work needed to be taken up early. As per his advice, we worked out the details and sent them to HQ for the necessary approval. The same was done after I left the project only and was completed later within the next few years. I was very happy that the most legitimate work for proper accommodation was ultimately completed.

Our company started an inter-project sports festival and that year it was organised at our Agartala plant. We had made our team ready for participation. As travelling from Doyang by road would take substantial time, I took special permission from the CEO to send the team by flight, and for most of our team members, it was their first air journey and they were so grateful to me. I was leading the team. Our team got several gold medals and on the final day of volleyball, our main player was very sick with a high fever. The doctor had given some injections to him and I was very worried about his health than the gold medal. But he forced me to allow him to play and I agreed. He played till the last point and we became the champion. That was a great honour for the entire Doyang team.

SPORTS

I was in Golaghat for a few days when a team of sportsmen from District Wokha came to my house on a courtesy visit. During discussions, we found that they had a good cricket team in the Wokha district and we decided that there should be a friendly cricket match between the Wokha district team and the Golaghat District team at our Doyang stadium. I discussed the matter with Golaghat cricket associations and they readily agreed. I requested the Chairman of the Golaghat Municipal Board to visit along with the team and he readily agreed. From our side, Dr. SS Choudhury who was a keen cricket lover was given the responsibility for all the arrangements. We sent our bus and two vehicles to Golaghat the previous night so that the Golaghat team could reach in the morning. They arrived quite early and we all had breakfast together before the match. The whole stadium was packed with our staff and local villagers. As far as I know, it was the first time such a match was organised between two neighbouring districts of Assam and Nagaland, which created a lot of goodwill between our people. Though the Golaghat team won by a few runs, all played with great sportsmanship. Medals or prizes were distributed by the Chairman GMB and our senior officers.

After the successful completion of the cricket match, Wokha People came to know about my interest in sports, and one day while I was in the office, the office-bearers of the Wokha district football association came to meet me. They organised a big football tournament every year, where a lot of teams participated from the state and it was very popular in the district. They told me to be the chief guest on the Final day. They also requested some contributions from our department but my financial power was very nominal and in such matters and if it were sent to HQ, they might not have got it that year. I told them frankly and they understood. Whatever money I could approve was given as a token of love for them. Later, I came to know that the big shots of the state gave huge amounts of donations to become the chief guest in that tournament. I was laughing and wondering on what basis they had honoured me by inviting me to be the Chief Guest. On that day, I along with all our senior project officers started for Wokha. Dr. Choudhury and Senior Engineer Patton were in my vehicle. In a flash, a thought came to my mind that if I could make the beginning of my speech in their Lotha dialect, it would be more effective. Dr. Choudhury knew the language and Patton himself was from the tribe. They drafted a few lines for me in their language but in the English alphabet so that I could read. These two were very naughty young men and always had smiling faces and were active in all project activities. I was not sure whether they had written correctly and whether what they had translated to me in English was something else altogether. After reaching there, I asked one of our officers the meaning of those sentences and I was assured that they were written nicely and correctly. There were people all around on the top of nearby buildings and trees and there was a big queue at the gate. I was welcomed by the officials from the gate in their traditional way, making me feel like a VIP. After the secretary introduced me to the public and requested me for a speech to the public, I stood up and started my speech in the language my colleague had written for me. When I finished my first two sentences, there was applause going on for quite a long time. It was my first experience speaking to such an open audience and getting their spontaneous applause made me crazy. I spoke for another few minutes and completed my speech. The game started. One of my closest friends from my school days was posted at Wokha in the SBI. He also came and joined me and after the match, we went to his house and enjoyed the evening. This was a great experience in my life that I will cherish it always. Next year, I sponsored the prizes but I was not there as I was transferred before the game.

I was sitting in my office one fine morning and a powerful businessman from Dimapur came to my chamber. We just started the initial welcome rituals of shaking hands and he had just taken his seat in front of me. Suddenly, about 20-25 villagers entered my room, which was guarded by security forces. One of them within a flash took out his *dao* or *Khukury* and straightway attacked the man and left the room. I could not even understand what had happened. It had pierced his hand near the shoulder and blood was coming out profusely, even some had fallen on my face and my shirt also. Blood was everywhere in my chamber. I called the doctor and he immediately did whatever was possible at the project hospital and I sent the gentleman to Dimapur for better treatment. It so happened that I could not even understand what was going on and by the time I got back to my senses, these people had left. I called the commandant and banged him left and right, knowing very well that even after my hard talk nothing positive would happen. We were keeping them as per government directive and we were unnecessarily taking the burden of their total expenditure.

***

I got a call from Mitu who was then posted in Delhi. She told me that she along with her husband wanted to visit our project as she never got the chance to visit the project earlier. She requested a vehicle at Guwahati airport so that they could come comfortably as she did not know how to come otherwise. I sent my vehicle to pick them up and kept a room for them at Golaghat Guest House. But they did not wait at Golaghat and reached Doyang post-midnight. The next day, I showed them the project and we had a boating in the reservoir to see the bridge as well. They were very happy with the beauty of the project and the fresh fish of Doyang reservoir. The next morning, they left for Guwahati on their way to Delhi. We had met after a long time and remembered our earlier days of working at Shillong. It was a great reunion.

INAUGURATION OF CHUBBY NALA BRIDGE

The work of the bridge was going on in full force and was nearly in the completion stage. We were planning the inauguration and the Chief Minister had earlier told us that he would visit to inaugurate the same. I asked my team to exclude one particular date as there was some very urgent personal work for me on that day.

One of my senior officers had gone to Shillong without my knowledge to meet the CEO and my boss. Both of them treated me as their enemy no. 1 and my few senior officers had informed them about the project in the way they liked without any professional ethics. He came back from Shillong via Kohima after meeting the CM and fixed a date, which I told him to exclude. I knew something fishy would definitely be happening and my intuitions had proved to be true. I cancelled my programme which was quite urgent and stayed there for the most discomfort of these people as they planned to perform the ceremony in my absence and make an issue out of it. The CEO and my immediate boss came one day ahead and I made an elaborate arrangement to welcome them and the welcome program was made by a few of my trusted men and not published to avoid any disruption from any quarter. It was a grand reception and some people were surprised to see how it was organised in such a traditional fashion without their knowledge. In the evening, I showed them the project, driving the vehicle by myself and avoiding the driver also. The CEO was an HR man and he had been fed with all kinds of technical issues in a way which met their intentions. A group of officers was very jealous about me performing the way they never thought I would and were very uncomfortable and tried to destabilise me from the beginning. A lot of problems came from various quarters internal as well as external. Their frustrations were coming out in their mouths sometimes very spontaneously. It was my dedication and my relations with my junior officers and my respect for the senior villagers that made me acceptable to them and they had given me a lot of love and respect. I owe my gratitude to all of them. They even used their contacts everywhere but every time, I was saved by the villagers and my employees. They knew me very well and that I did not know anything else other than the works of the project and the employees' and the village people's welfare. I got threatened several times and every time, the villagers and the employees saved me. The immediate boss who was supposed to be the main technical advisor to the CEO was feeding him with all kinds of misinformation.

After the visit of the CEO, he came to know the actual situation as I took him to all the places and explained everything in minute detail and the other so-called technical experts had to keep their mouths shut. The CEO was very impressed and he and I had a confidential meeting at the guest house after dinner.

The next morning, all the arrangements were made ready but as there was rain the previous night, the road that was yet to be blacktopped was becoming muddy. However, the inauguration was completed successfully by the Chief Minister and six or seven cabinet ministers attended the meeting along with our CEO.

After going back, my immediate boss issued me an explanation call letter with all the fictitious charges. Earlier, when I got such letters, I never gave them any importance and put them in my dustbin as I had more important work to do than attending to such unproductive correspondences. But this time he crossed the limit and so, I decided to reply. I replied to him with information to all Directors and the CEO and told him to substantiate the charges or I would consider it a mala fide or intentional to hurt me which he never replied. Certain people in a company are raised to a level where they are not supposed to be and because of their incompetence, they become restless when somebody below them performs and prove to be better than them. That is the reason that in earlier letters, I did not even reply but this time this was too much after a grand ceremony where the whole state machinery, including our top management, participated and openly praised our work. I invited all the outgoing HOPs to the inauguration function and all praised our teams.

The CEO understood that the relationship between me and my boss was not repairable and he transferred me to Shillong under a different ED who was looking after thermal and transmission. Amarjit was to replace me.

Amarjit was in Shillong and I told him not to vacate his house and that I would take that house on rent as getting a house was very difficult in Shillong. His house was located in a good locality and was a good independent house within the campus of the owner with enough parking space.

BACK TO SHILLONG

NEW AREA OF WORK IN SHILLONG

So, after reaching Shillong, my first job was to meet the house owner and occupy the house. All were settled and my furniture also arrived. Amarjit was engaging a lady for cleaning and cooking, the same lady met me and I very happily appointed her to do these jobs. In my new office, my workload was quite substantial and I used to come very late. So, I kept one of my house keys with her and kept some money so that whatever is required she used to market herself. She was very particular about giving me the account every week.

I was a bit relaxed as she looked after all my household staff. The house was reasonably big and families could also come and stay comfortably there.

Our AGTP gas plant was running in open cycle mood due to the non-availability of sufficient perennial source of surface water body near to the plant and air-cooled condensing technology was not there at the time of planning of the project. But in the meantime, air-cooled condensing technology was developed and that reduced the requirement of water and there were several manufacturers in the market with this technology. We were losing the generation from the exhaust hot gases from the gas turbine that could be utilised for power generation through steam turbine. We planned to convert this plant into a combined cycle plant by putting steam turbine using air-cooled condenser technology. One firm was engaged in the preparations of DPR. After several rounds of modification, the same was finalised and sent for Clearance to our technical consultant. There also, we were required to make certain modifications prior to getting their clearances. My new ED gave me full liberty and I had to frequently travel to Delhi to get the DPR cleared by concerned authorities and after their clearance, submitted it to the Ministry as it requires approval of the Ministry. As the investment was not much, the approval did not require cabinet approval and could be given by the empowered committee called EFC headed by secretary. The joint secretary Finance of the ministry had some observations which we had met. Mitu was that time posted in Delhi and we two were running from here and there to get the clearances. We felt it would be better to meet all the members of the committee before the meeting and we met them all and reached the office around 12:30 when we were told to meet Director Tech of a CPSU as the joint Secretary finance of the ministry did not have full faith in our clarification and requested his view. We went there and met him. He was very sharp and after a glance at the paper, he asked us a few questions. He was satisfied and told us to go ahead. I requested him to call the JS (F) so that he could also be convinced. He talked to him in our presence and the meeting was held on time. Within a few minutes, the meeting was over and the project was cleared. The construction started shortly and was commissioned. But none felt that we should also be a part of the inauguration function. We brought the project facing all the difficulties and with all our effort or initiatives, the project had seen the light. But normally such a thought never happened. I remembered the Kopili reservoir acidity issue that was detected by us and we did all the groundwork, including documentation and after my transfer from the project, an all-India conference was organised but I came to know about it after it was over. People had used papers prepared by us to show how diligent they were. Life is like that. Some people enjoy doing something by themselves without waiting for recognition and others take all the credit for the work of others. Till you are required, you are important and after that, you are a burden. Since such things were routine with me, by this time I hardly cared for such happenings.

The Turial project in Mizoram was coming but the evacuation line that was constructed by Mizoram Power department from Kolasib to the project site was not ready. I went to Kolasib with my colleague Peter and met the Executive Engineer. We had to camp for a few days there to complete the job, which was basically delayed because of a lack of coordination between the project team and the power department.

By that time, my ED retired and our department's name was changed to Planning, which was headed by an officer I worked together with in Kameng HEP. He, being a civil engineer and about to retire, had given all the work to me only. During that time, I had made a proposal to have a solar power plant in the excess land we had at our Monarchak project in Tripura on an experimental basis, which was agreed but the tendering and execution had taken quite a long time. However, it came out successfully and was the first MW sized solar plant in the entire North East. Other big CPSUs also entered the solar power field after us. Why we could not progress in solar would be a totally different chapter but we were competent to do much better and could have been a leader in this field. By this time, I took over as Executive Director (Planning).

There were various hydro projects we were looking for execution in the coming years. We were studying the future potential of those projects and their techno-economic viability. One of them was studied properly by our team and we did not find the project as viable techno-commercially. Accordingly, I placed a note to my director and he sent back the file to me with his initials only without any comment, so I thought he agreed to my proposal. I closed the file and kept it in the cabinet. However, after a few months, the State Government desired that we should take over the project for executions. Our new CEO was very eager to do the project and asked for the file. I showed him the file and he was very annoyed as there was no ground on which he could overrule my noting and take the project. As a result, on the same day a new post of ED Renewable Energy was created and I was shifted there.

In the meantime, the corporation was trying to implement ERP (Enterprise Resource Planning) and a few times, the tenders were made unsuccessfully. The CEO called me to his chamber and told me to additionally take over the charge of the Information technology department and to go ahead in these directions. I told my Boss who recently took over that I am ready if I would be given a free hand. He agreed. Accordingly, one consultant was appointed and we made the specification ready but one department had intentionally tried to derail the project and had it delayed in every step. Ultimately, the tender was floated and none participated. We were disappointed but we knew as to why it failed as certain conditions were put by certain departments that nobody was interested in. I immediately, with the permission of the CEO, made a pre-tender discussion with the probable bidders in Delhi and we were very happy to have wide participation. We noted their views and incorporated those whichever were practical and legally valid and the tender was again floated. It was very shameful that some departments were taking months after months to evaluate the tender and written whatever they wish in the file making it difficult for our contract department to award the contract. There were no actions against those people. During my entire career, I have noticed that one bad element in the team can destroy the efforts of all the other sincere people and serious actions were necessary in those cases. The CEO was also a very soft person and he did not take a strong stand. Ultimately, we had taken the advice of a third-party evaluation and the work was finally awarded. We had crossed the first hurdle successfully even though it was substantially delayed.

By that time, we had completed the Monarchak solar plant of 5MW and had already gained some experience. The Government of India had also given a lot of emphasis on renewables and we had a lot of work coming. Unlike some other companies, we had some major limitations as the area of North East India did not have much solar potential as radiation level was low and due to the unavailability of wasteland. Whatever free land was available, all were fertile agricultural land and could not be used for solar projects so we had to go out of northeast India to have solar capacity additions. As a government entity, we had a lot of difficulty in land acquisitions and the procedures were quite cumbersome. The government policy of bundling of the excess power over-allocated power made some other entities in more competitive positions as their overall tariff came down and we did not have that advantage. With all those constraints, we decided to have a joint venture with a manufacturer of solar panels. By that time, a new corporation SECI (Solar power corporation of India) was formed and they had gone for tendering with viability gap funding (VGF). Whoever needed lower VGF, they got the project. We participated in that tender with our joint venture partner and got a 50 MW project to be executed in Madhya Pradesh.

The project was a test for us and we did the project within the scheduled completion time. This was, to the best of my knowledge, the first public-private partnership which successfully completed the solar project on time. The project was very beautifully made and we gained enough expertise doing this project. Thereafter we participated as JV in other tenders also and got another 2X25 MW in Andhra Pradesh, the first project was completed and there was some delay in the second project due to land acquisition issues. In the meantime, we had decided to empanel some manufacturers and erectors for bidding of our own. With this model, we submitted two bids and in both bids, we were short-listed but in the reverse bidding process, we lost as some very absurd prices were quoted by a few private firms against which we couldn't compete in any case. But both the time, we were in the race till the last moment and we were the only power sector PSU that participated in the bidding process and put up a fight till the last minute. Within the last few years, the solar price had come down from Rs 14.00 to Rs 2.24 per unit and the market was very volatile. Those states that came first had high tariffs and the states that came later got lower tariffs. These made the states scared to sign power purchase agreements with any developer and we had to gradually come out of the race for some time. We had started an investigation of wind power potentials but commercial viability was not there in the NE.

In the meantime, Mitu who was posted at Guwahati in the Design wing got transferred to my office. We two visited almost all the states to find out opportunities in the solar sector. We got an offer at Odisha for a 200 Mw project. Immediately, we jumped onto the job and got all the clearances. With the appointment of a consultant from Bhubaneswar itself, who was one of the most respected Engineers of Odisha, we identified the land and as the land in Odisha was to be taken only through the government department, there were not many formalities. We were very hopeful about the project. Unfortunately, by that time our CEO retired, and our new CEO and new Director were not at all interested in the solar projects. This project, after all the clearances, including the comfort letter of power purchase from the state, could not be taken forward as the management's involvement was not there from the beginning. Even after we fixed a few meetings with the top bureaucrats and the Ministers, those were to be cancelled because of the non-availability of our Top Management at the last moment. This had put us in a very awkward position and the state government officials who were so favourable to us were not willing to give us the project later. The coffin was closed.

Our head of security who was a Brigadier rank officer on deputation had to go back after his term completed. Considering my experience related to security, I was given the additional charge of Safety and Security of the corporation. It was a huge responsibility and I became busy from morning till late. Mitu and I always took our tiffin together in my room and she brought something and I brought something, which we both shared and she was calling me almost every day as I was moving around all the offices. After a few days, even after my repeated protest, the commercial department was also given to me. I told my Director and the CEO that it was simply impossible for me to concentrate on all the responsibilities and all the department would suffer. The department of Renewables, Information Technology Safety and Security, and Commercial were all critical departments and for one man running all the four critical departments meant that all the departments would suffer.

After a few months, I was relieved from Commercial but Mitu who was helping me in renewables was shifted to Commercial. We had shared our responsibilities together for the Renewables but after her transfer to Commercial, I needed to give more time in RE.

I thought that since her promotions were due that was why she must have been placed there but I was wrong as in the next interview, she was not promoted. I really felt bad.

She was a lady capable of taking a lot of responsibility and always got involved in whatever was given to her. While she was in my office, we worked as a team and she shared the workload equally with me without any complaints. That helped me to give more time to the IT department and the Security and Safety department. When I had taken over IT, our sites were connected with VSAT at a very high cost which was of 0.5 mb capacity to 2 Mb capacity. I gradually changed the complete network with MPLS leased line and all sites were happy to have high-speed internet. This was a must prior to implementation of ERP in our corporation.

Our share in the solar joint venture company was sold to the other partner and now we came back again to an installed capacity of 5 MW only in the solar field. What a shame for a company! A leader can lift a company with his foresight and decision-making capacity and also can finish an organisation without any idea about which way they should move while keeping themselves busy with matters that can be taken care of by their juniors. At that level, technical knowledge was secondary to making policy decisions fast. The world within the last one decade has changed and those who cannot compete will vanish. So, quick decision-making and putting the company in a race with their competitors were vital, instead of keeping busy with things which could have been very well delegated to one's juniors. It is very easy to blame one another but very difficult to have a self-analysis, which is where one fails. Another aspect I always emphasise to my superiors is the tendency to generalise any issue. One performer should not suffer at the cost of the non-performers as that creates a lot of resentment amongst the hard workers and demoralises them. But it is always the other way: those for whatever quality except for performance become close to the top and are always rewarded.

KICK-OFF MEETING ON ERP

After the successful award of the ERP tender to a firm by our contract department, the execution was responsibly given to the IT department and I was placed as the overall in charge. The kick-off meeting was held in Delhi, where all very senior-level officials of our consultant, review consultant, the OEM, and the top officials of the system integrators were present. Our CEO and all directors also participated. The IT team and the Contract and Finance team also joined the meeting through video conferencing from Shillong. The meeting was going on very smoothly but suddenly one of our senior most officials who had created a lot of problems in the proposal of implementation of the ERP in the corporation created a nuisance in the meeting and everyone was very offended. The CEO left the meeting. Other outside officials were feeling very much insulted with the way this man had proven himself in the open meeting about his ignorance and such behaviour from a high-level officer was so humiliating to all the participants, especially to me as the project in charge and to a few of the country heads of the participants. I went to the Director technical who was chairing the meeting at that time to stop the meeting to save all from further embarrassment. The meeting was over. It was a scene I never witnessed again in my 30-plus years of service. It was total indecency in such a crucial meeting and I was so ashamed that after the meeting, I personally met all our guests and apologised for his misbehaviour. It was late and one of my colleagues and I went to a nearby park to cool our heads and was walking barefoot on the grass for some time before coming back to our hotel to have a few pegs before having dinner. The next day morning, I left for Shillong via Guwahati as my family and my younger son, who had come home after his final examination, was there. Next day in the office, I kept myself busy in helping my IT team for a presentation the next day as we had introduced a knowledge-sharing programme to all the employees and this time it was our turn. That was a Friday and a beautiful presentation was made by my team. It was late when I returned home. Mitu was with me and I dropped her off at her residence. I was also a bit tired because of that particular meeting which was so nasty. The behaviour of the senior officer made us ashamed in front of so many organisations that were present there and my anger was still not gone. After coming back to Shillong, all were talking about how during their career such behaviour and nonsensical words were never heard even though we have arguments and counter-arguments always but decency was always maintained.

I was sleeping quite late in the morning and in the evening, I went to the market with my son to purchase chicken, which he was very fond of and we prepared the same and had it and it was very tasty. I went to bed but after I was in bed, I felt very uncomfortable. I thought it was a problem with gastritis and took medicine for that but I was not feeling better. After some time, I started vomiting. I thought that then I would be okay and told my wife to go to bed and I was sitting for some time. My son wanted to take me to the hospital but I was not interested as I had no such ailment and a few months back, I had my annual health check-up done. Moreover, sometime back I was also in Ladakh at 18000 ft for more than 15 days as a part of an inter-ministerial and inter CPSU combine team regarding renewable energy projects there and a DPR for 5000 MW solar at Ladakh and 2500 in Kargil was earlier made under my leadership.

But gradually again, I was feeling uncomfortable. My son called my driver who was staying nearby and we went to the hospital emergency. They did some tests and told me that I already had a severe heart attack and I should shift to another hospital as there was no cardiologist in that hospital. I was quite normal and I told my son that this time it seems to be tough. I did not remember going to the hospital or seeing the doctor except for my yearly medical check-up, which was mandatory in my corporation. I went straight to that hospital and by that time, I was feeling some difficulty in my breathing. They put me in the ICU and under a ventilator. The treatment had started and the young doctors were taking good care of me. Angiography and angioplasty were supposed to be done but due to some internal problem in the hospital, that was not done and I was discharged after 14 days of stay there. I came back home but the next morning, I again felt the breathlessness and I called the driver and started for Guwahati, where there were better medical facilities. After going down the hill towards Guwahati, gradually I felt much better and we decided that I should better move directly to Delhi and booked our ticket online and reached Delhi airport without any problem and straightway went to the hospital. We met the senior doctor and he, immediately after examining me, talked with some other doctors and decided to go ahead with angiography that day itself and sent me to OT where angiography was done. Everything was going very fast. Dr. Atul Mathur introduced himself and did the procedure and then I was shifted to the ICU. I was in good condition except for the fact that the oxygen supply was there. But suddenly, I collapsed and I did not know what had happened except that I was hearing some murmurs and I understood there were a lot of senior doctors attending to me. Maybe after an hour, I came back to my senses and all seemed to be relieved. But again, after some time, I lost my senses. The doctors were quite worried. But this time also, I came back after maybe an hour. The doctors were concerned. I saw the echo and some other machine near me and I was fully under observation. The doctor told me that all my parameters were normal but why such things were happening, they could not understand. The angioplasty that was scheduled for the next day was deferred till I got stabilised and they told me all was well. By then, my son was near me. Normally, no one is allowed but as my condition deteriorated, he was allowed. Angioplasty was supposed to be done the next day but considering my condition, it was deferred by a day and successfully done. I was better and discharged within the next two days. We stayed at our guest house but after the second day, I was again experiencing breathlessness and I was admitted in an emergency. They found some problem with my Mitral valve but decided not to operate and with medicine, I became stable within a few days and was discharged. After a few days, on the day of Ashtami puja day of *Ma Durga* (I am a devotee of *Ma Durga* and I get strength from her whenever I am in trouble), we all went to a Puja mandap and prayed. My son came back with me while my daughter and wife stayed back for some more time. As soon as they came back, I was having serious breathlessness and again required to be admitted to emergency. This time, doctors were not taking any risk and all necessary tests were carried out. They found that the lower point pivot of my Mitral valve was damaged and the valve required replacement. I was in the ICU. One more day, I went totally unconscious and came back after an hour. The doctors were trying to go for open heart surgery to replace the valve but my lung was dilated and so it was delayed. Every morning, they took an X-ray and after a week or so, they finally decided to go for the operation. In the evening, the surgeon and his team came and explained to me that they were planning the operation the next day and briefed the whole process to me. The senior-most surgeon was not talking but was looking at me in my eyes. He must be sixty-plus but was looking young and slim. Then he asked me if I had any questions. I said since I am in the best hands, I have nothing to ask but want to know normally what the time of recovery is. He was laughing and told me that it depended on me. If I am bold and think positive, I will be back home shortly. They left.

Next day, I was made ready and they allowed my family members to meet me and I was taken to the Special OT. Most probably, all major heart surgery was done there. After some time, I found that many doctors, technicians, and nurses were in and I was given an injection after which I did not know what was happening.

***

After the successful operation and after a few days' stay in the ICU, I was shifted to the cabin where only one person from the family was allowed. I was recovering well and the doctors confirmed that after various tests being done on a regular basis; yet, I was physically very weak and I lost a lot of weight. Soon I shifted to my rented house, which my daughter and son had found for me and we took it for rent for two months. During that period, I had to be in the hospital for various reasons but gradually, I was feeling better. I went for the regular check-ups as advised and after two months, the doctors allowed me to go back home with a recommendation that I should be near a place where a tertiary cardio facility was available. I forwarded the same to my CEO and he was kind enough to allow me to function from Guwahati and on my request, all other Departments except for Information Technology were handed over to other senior officers.

We booked our return ticket for the entire family and reached the airport.

***

I did not believe in astrology as I have not studied the matter or ever consulted an astrologist. During my stay in the hospital, my family was consulting some astrologers who had no idea about me or my family but they had clearly explained to them my health conditions accurately, which made me think about learning the subject after my retirement.

***

I woke up suddenly from my sleep with the announcement made by the air hostess to bind our seatbelts and that the weather ahead was bad; the heavy turbulence must have woken me up. After some time, the turbulence was over and everything was getting back to normal. The flight was gradually descending for landing at the Guwahati airport.

I became fully awake. My kids and wife were worried all along the flight but fortunately, I was sleeping the whole time and enjoying my dreams. They were relieved that ultimately, we all had safely landed at Guwahati.

Sheru, my driver, was waiting at the front of the arrival lounge and he was so happy to welcome us back and carried our luggage to the car. I saw tears coming out of his eyes and he tried to hide it from me. A long turbulent journey was over and I saw the beautiful smile on Sheru's face to welcome me back.

I thanked God and everyone who was with me and had prayed for me during these turbulent journeys of ups and downs throughout my life.

A few months back, I visited the Doyang Hydro Electric project. There is now a two-lane highway without any unscientific gradient and the area where people used to run to see our jeeps have turned into a posh area with people who own luxury cars. Machinery for handling heavy consignments is available there for rent. Doyang project is now connected with high-speed internet and 4G mobile service by various service providers. I was really so happy to see all these positive developments. Few of the villagers, now quite old, came to meet me and hugged me, which made me really emotional.

A new chapter in my life has started totally different from the life I was used to for the last 36 years.

www.ingramcontent.com/pod-product-compliance
Lightning Source LLC
Chambersburg PA
CBHW060914140726
47996CB00001B/242